GW00601681

Dear Val,

Happy Christmas 2014

Lots of

Love

Martin

xx x

NOMAD
BRINGING YOUR TRAVELS HOME

SIBELLA COURT

MURDOCH BOOKS

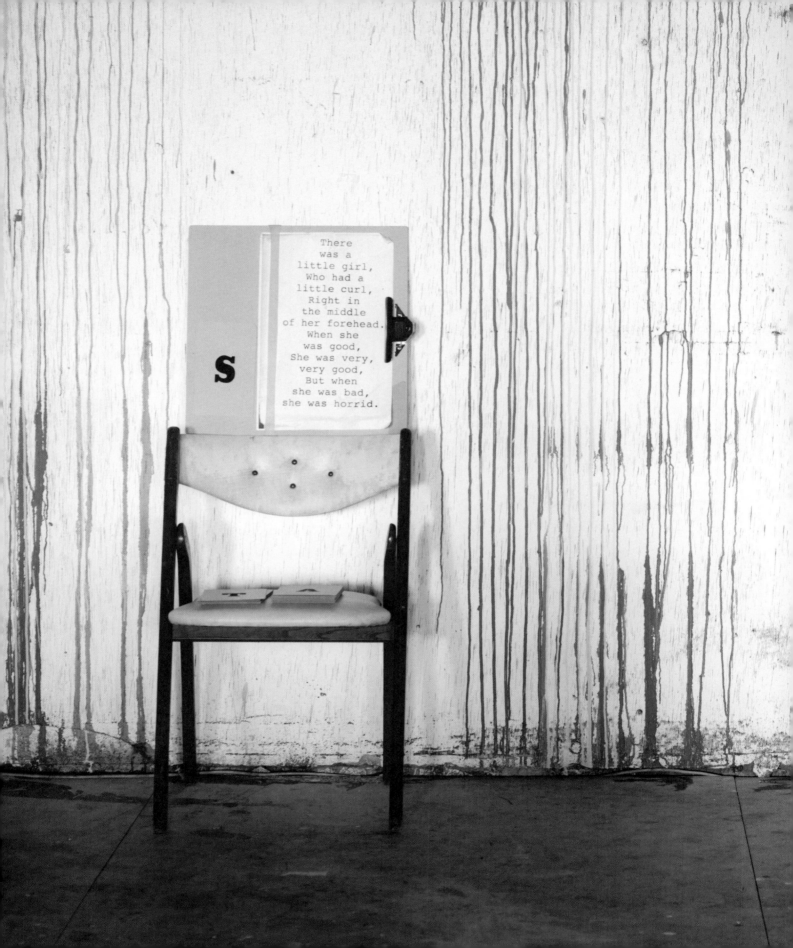

CONTENTS

INTRODUCTION 6

JAPAN 18

ITALY 58

INDIA 102

SYRIA 148

MEXICO 198

MY REFERENCE
LIBRARY 242

SHOPS &
THINGS I LOVE 248

HOTELS I
STAYED IN 250

COOL PLACES 252

THANK YOU 255

HOW TO USE THE BOOK

Holidays are too few and far between. To have a piece of that experience and memory reflected in your interior — even the smallest incidental that makes you smile and takes you to another place — is what it's all about. This book is to excite and motivate you. Please use it accordingly, and feel free to borrow my ideas, or use them to inspire your own. There are no mistakes, only journeys. Every time I travel I really, really want something: For instance, in Japan it was the interconnecting internal rooms and gardens of houses changed by shoji screens. In Italy it was the Fiat 500! (cream with tan interior for me, please) and in India, it was overscaled formal photographs of mostly men, lots of them sporting magnificent moustaches, in safari hats and turbans in front of estates.

Although I can't bring all the things I really want back with me, I still find plenty of inspiration that's easily adapted and incorporated into my life, and home. I'm going to let you know how I do it — with lots of my globetrotting inspiration pics and notes from my travels, and pages and pages of shots to show you how I adapt ideas from them, usually quite simply, for use at home. You don't have to follow those ideas exactly, but they should give you some idea of how my mind works, the sorts of things that inspire me, and the way those things can be shifted and shaken up, adapted and transformed, and still manage to capture experiences and memories.

To be able to share your laughs and travel frustrations (which are often funnier) in a 'remember that' kind of way is a clever, emotive way to treat your interior and be surrounded by the things you love. It's about your stories reflecting your life.

TAKING PICS

You can't be expected to store all your travel experiences in your head — you'll need a few photos to jog your memory. But you don't need to be a professional photographer to take a great pic. With a little confidence and some patience you can get a fantastic picture.

It's all about composition.

Consider what's in your frame, adopt a stylist's eye for crop and angle. Work out what should and shouldn't be in the pic. Check, for example, where a wall or stair ends, or that you're getting in the top of an object. To avoid distortion, it can sometimes be a good idea to stand back and zoom in; likewise, you need to be careful not to stand at an odd angle, otherwise things can look as if they're tilting. Take your time — a snapshot doesn't have to be 'snap', but it can still look spontaneous.

The beauty of digital is you can check everything and go back to correct, right then and there.

It's important to edit; be ruthless and do it
as you go along, before you download your pics.
It makes for a stronger 'story' at the end,
which often gets neglected upon your return.

Don't store your photos away — I get mine
printed as soon as I get back. It keeps the
globetrotting inspirations alive as well as let
me physically move the pics around, put them
in a different order, and play with colour and
content. You'll find this plays a large part in
coming up with a trip-based 10-colour palette
(more on that on page 17), even if one wasn't
obvious while you were gallivanting around.

I often think of pictures in pagination,
i.e. how the pages turn and a story runs in a
magazine. I like to make a strong picture story
of it, which can then be put into an album if
I feel like it.

By doing all these things, inspiration and
excitement from your trip should be at the
forefront of your mind and you are ready to
experiment with your own interior.

9

WHO I AM

I AM
A TREASURE HUNTER,
BEACHCOMBER AND
BOWERBIRD.
I AM A DESIGNER OF
HARDWARE, AMONG OTHER
THINGS. I CREATE SPACES
& INTERIORS.
I TALK IN PAIRS AND
WRITE WITH AMPERSANDS:
BITS & BOBS,
HABERDASHERY
& HARDWARE,
TRAVELLERS & MERCHANTS.
I AM A NAMER OF
PAINTS.
I AM A GYPSY,
A GLOBETROTTER AND
EXPLORER, BUT LOVE
TO COME HOME.
I AM LO-FI.

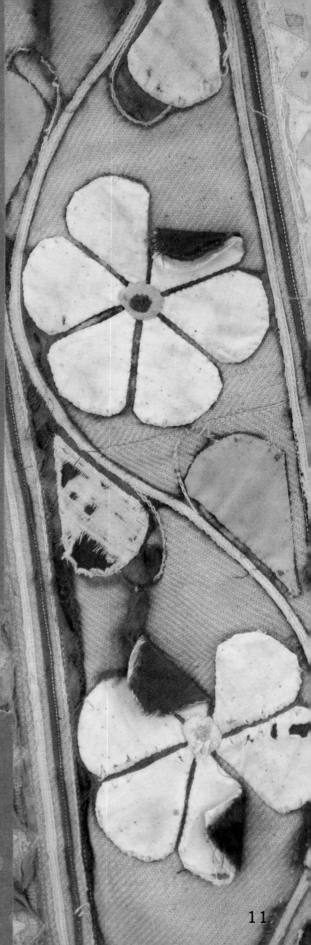

INSPIRATION

I hadn't travelled to most of these places before,
but they were all in my top 15 (don't you have a list
of countries you want to travel to?) The reason I
chose these five for the book was that I thought
I wouldn't be the only person who'd want to go to
them — they were the sorts of places that other
people would have on their wish lists or would have
been to already. I picked countries or places that
were diverse in culture, religion, adventure and
geography, the idea being that they would reveal
themselves in very different ways. I was right:
even in colour terms, there were the desert tones
of dusty Damascus, the serpent scale tones of the
Amalfi Coast, the deep indigos of Japanese papers
and textiles, the pops of reds and fuchsia in the
flowers in Mexico City, the faded dirty pales of
painted woodwork in India. Inspiration comes in
many shapes and forms, and often not literally.

I did not go looking for existing interiors to
re-create when I returned home, but wanted to draw
from all aspects of my trips: a street sign, a garden
grate, a leaf on wet cobblestone, washing drying
against a painted wall, a glimpse into a foreign
kitchen, the mundane and the fancy.

Don't rule out the casual walk around a new town
as a source of inspiration, as well as museums,
restaurants, shops: experience it all and do as I
do, and take lots of pictures. I am always attracted
to the unusual and the curious, and hunt them out in
daily food markets, monthly flea and antique markets
(preferably the outdoor ones, with goods spilling out
of the back of vans!), natural history museums, both
small and large, artists' ateliers, historic houses
and traders' workshops etc. The appeal of old trades
and crafts that still exist from textile dyers and
embroiderers, shell arts, wood turners and mills,
paper makers, smiths and tinkers, foundries, leather
workers and tanneries, felters, basket weavers etc
are always at the forefront of any of my exploring
both across the globe and in my local environment.

STYLING VS DECORATING

I shot all the styling ideas at locations around
Sydney (thank you to all my friends!) with my
brother, Chris. It shows that you can use any
decorative background and restyle and change,
according to your desires and recent inspirations.
Any of these locations could have been changed to
suit any of my travel inspirations. This book is
not about theming but rather adding flavour from
your recent globetrotting adventures.

It's about displaying your souvenirs or just
your memories through colour, installation and
imagination to reveal your inspirations, nomadic
spirit and own personality. Note: if you are unable
to travel physically, you can still take journeys
and be inspired via reading, movies, magazines,
books and your general interests.

This book is not about expensive renovations
or construction changes, but about adding and
subtracting and rearranging of your existing
things, it's about lo-fi and being clever and
upcycling with the things you already have.
Note: these are two new words I'm testing out that
I think are relevant and you, too, should know.

Upcycling is to reclaim, reuse, recycle;
to give old materials/furniture/products a new
lease of life.

Lo-fi originates from the music/sound world.
However, in my world it means low expense, and
achieving, with ease and casual abandon, a relaxed
liveable space that reflects your personality
and lifestyle.

The ideas can be as simple as creating a new
'art wall', which you can add to and subtract
from, with postcards, invitations, photocopies
of designs you like or pages torn from magazines;
growing new flowers in your window box, layering
different textures on your bed, hanging a new piece
of fabric over your window, or changing the colour
of your floor or walls. All things that exist in
your current environment — it's just a matter of
seeing things in a new way.

TRAVELLING COMPANIONS

For me, the excitement of a new place is of all
the senses being challenged: to not know the
language or the lay of the land, to be bombarded
by new scents, climates and flavours.

For this book, I travelled on my own and with
various travel companions along the way and
enjoy how their personalities and expectations
mould the travel story. Most of my trips had
at least dual purposes, which took me into
factories, basements and manufacturers among
many other places. I travelled for the book,
obviously, but also to buy stuff for my shop, The
Society Inc; to develop new product ranges; for
inspiration with Anthropologie; and for holidays
— we all need those.

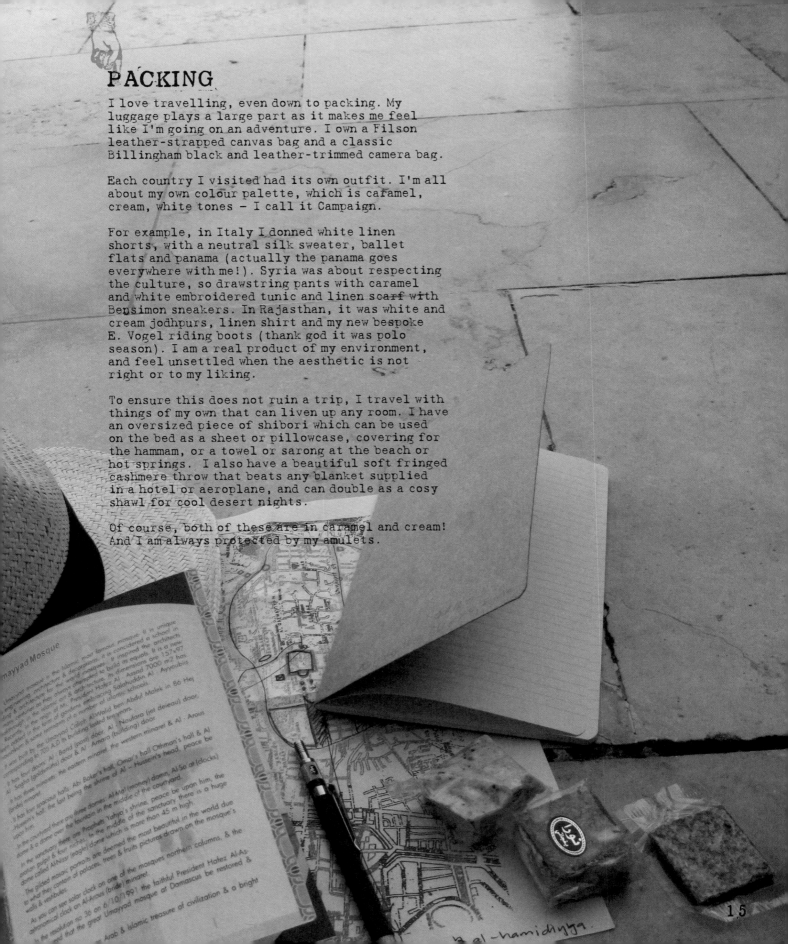

PACKING

I love travelling, even down to packing. My luggage plays a large part as it makes me feel like I'm going on an adventure. I own a Filson leather-strapped canvas bag and a classic Billingham black and leather-trimmed camera bag.

Each country I visited had its own outfit. I'm all about my own colour palette, which is caramel, cream, white tones – I call it Campaign.

For example, in Italy I donned white linen shorts, with a neutral silk sweater, ballet flats and panama (actually the panama goes everywhere with me!). Syria was about respecting the culture, so drawstring pants with caramel and white embroidered tunic and linen scarf with Bensimon sneakers. In Rajasthan, it was white and cream jodhpurs, linen shirt and my new bespoke E. Vogel riding boots (thank god it was polo season). I am a real product of my environment, and feel unsettled when the aesthetic is not right or to my liking.

To ensure this does not ruin a trip, I travel with things of my own that can liven up any room. I have an oversized piece of shibori which can be used on the bed as a sheet or pillowcase, covering for the hammam, or a towel or sarong at the beach or hot springs. I also have a beautiful soft fringed cashmere throw that beats any blanket supplied in a hotel or aeroplane, and can double as a cosy shawl for cool desert nights.

Of course, both of these are in caramel and cream! And I am always protected by my amulets.

THE 10-COLOUR PALETTE

As you may know from my first book, *Etcetera*,
I believe in working with a 10-colour palette.
I've found this to be the best starting point for
decorating a space. I don't necessarily use every
colour in the palette – I might only use a couple
or I might use half a dozen – but it creates a
framework for me, giving me the freedom to play
with the mood of a room or house, and ensures a
unified end result.

Each country I visited for this book gradually
revealed its own palette as I took in my
surroundings - the palette can come from
everywhere and anywhere. The colour of raw
leather in a cobbler's studio, of a doorknob
or a fish scale, of a flower in a roadside shrine
or a flash of graffiti on a laneway wall.

I always give names to my 10-colour palettes.
Here they are:
• North by Northwest for Japan
• Tales of a Sea Gypsy for Italy
• Objet Trouve for India
• Merchants & Traders for Syria
• Tender is the Night for Mexico.

As well, I have Foundation, which works as a
base neutral 10-colour palette, complementing
any colour choices, but also a complete option
in its own right. You can find more about it
in *Etcetera*.

Feel free to use any of my colours, but when
you're travelling, you'll find you come up
with your own. Make a note of what appeals to
you — it could be an old poster on a lamppost,
the label on an aperitif bottle behind the bar,
a broken bucket. Pick up mementoes as you go;
most won't come from souvenir shops. A packet
of wooden pegs might grab your attention, or
a buoy from a lobster pot, a barber's pole
drinking straw or an old-fashioned card game.
Take snaps of everything you see — once you get
home, shuffle and lay down your favourite pics
and mementoes on the table, keep adding and
subtracting and eventually you'll see colour
patterns emerging, which you can then form into
your own 10-colour palette.

There are no right or wrong combinations —
it's your interior and it's a matter of working
out what makes you happy. Most of the time, a
harmonious palette can be achieved, one that
will become the basis for your decorating
adventures. You'll be able to use the colours
in different combinations. Some rooms will
be peaceful and subtle, and you'll go for the
softer, more neutral tones. The more social
spaces can be a bit more energetic — denser
in colour, louder in pattern and texture.

郵便
POST

Delica

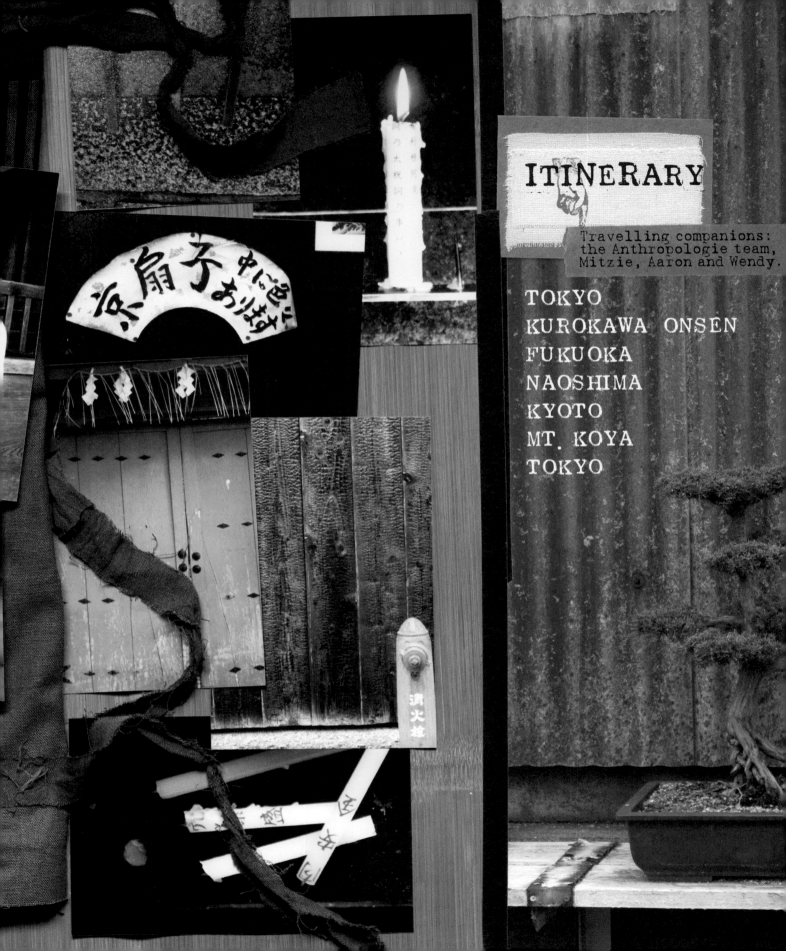

ITINeRARY

Travelling companions:
the Anthropologie team,
Mitzie, Aaron and Wendy.

TOKYO
KUROKAWA ONSEN
FUKUOKA
NAOSHIMA
KYOTO
MT. KOYA
TOKYO

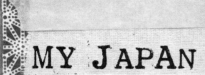

MY JAPAN

HANDMADE

I have a large collection of all things
Japanese handmade. Not only textiles, but
wooden combs with long stems, paintbrushes
made of feathers, carved seals with tiny
round red ink pads, woven travelling sake
cups, metal letterpress pieces, wrapped
stones, tea ceremony ladles, bone and ebony
game pieces, hand-thrown ceramic cups &
bowls, calligraphy books, brooms & cleaning
brushes, mini gardening tools, reed woven
slippers, copper tulip shaped rainchains etc.

My mother was very good at adding to this
ever-growing collection of bits and pieces.

All these precious things fit into my very
romantic view of Japan: firefly-lit paper
lanterns, intricate seasonal kimonos, wooden
shoes on cobblestone streets, kingfisher
hairpins, sitting cross-legged on a tatami
mat practising calligraphy or preparing for
the tea ceremony.

[THIS PAGE]
An unusual curtain tie back
that looks like an oversized
hair ornament a geisha might
use on a casual day.

MODERN JAPAN

Naoshima was established as an art island in
the South of Japan. The Benesse House and Chichu
Art Museum, designed by Tadao Ando, had been on my
list for a long time.

Going to a purpose-built and designed art space
on an island in the Seto Inland Sea was such a pure
experience. It's called the Art House Project
and is made up of scattered buildings and site-
specific sculptures, old and new.

Art and museums make up a big part of my travel
inspiration and itinerary.

Noguchi, a Japanese-American, is one of my
all-time favourite artists. There's an amazing
Noguchi museum in Long Island City, New York, that
I have visited so many times, and was curious to
see how Modern Japan sat with the Edo style I love
so much.

PAPER

One of my true passions is paper: stationery, lanterns, fans,
kites, books, packaging, origami, woodblocked sheets, indigo dyed,
stencils, bags, tags of all descriptions, plates & cups, envelopes,
notebooks, string, confetti, card — you name it, I love it.

And the Japanese crafters who make all these things: paper lanterns
with shop names hand-painted on them; the large, over-sized sheets
that look like lace, or have leaves embedded in them; the simplicity
of a classic diamond-shaped kite or the complexity of a moving,
flying dragon; the festivity of streaming multi-coloured street
decorations; lacquered all-weather umbrellas paper-pasted on a
bamboo skeleton; the feather-weight of the finest mulberry paper,
bound and stitched, for practising calligraphy; the crunchiness
of gold leaf-backed ancient scroll housed in its own balsawood box
and the intricate patterned squares for origami. As you can see, I
embrace all things paper.

Your eyes tel
me everything
I need to kno

Don't speak.
Just let me
look at you.

LOOSE LIPS
MIGHT
SINK SHIPS

ArGO
COOPERATIVA
GUARDIE NOTTURNE GIU...
Via A. Scialoia N° 10 - Tel. 244...
2345333 5 linee interne

I WAS BORN ON A PIRATE SHIP

HISTOIRE NATURELLE   HISTOIRE NATURELLE

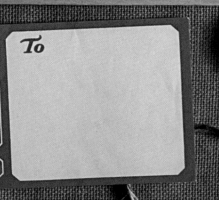

Contents - MERCHANDISE
POSTMASTER: THIS PARCEL
MAY BE OPENED FOR POSTAL
INSPECTION IF NECESSARY

—FROM—
Sibella Court
120 Walker Street
4th Floor
Chinatown NYC 10013

RETURN POSTAGE
GUARANTEED

To

ATLAS
ATLAS

earnest sewn

BORO & SHIBORI

My good friends Karman and Paul who own Edo Arts in Sydney started my love of boro many years ago. Boro is a well-worn, pre-loved-many-times patched indigo fabric usually found in sheet-like sizes used for covering futons.

It is a peasant fabric and definitely not museum worthy. However, that's the appeal of it. The mends, the patches, the stitches — the more the merrier! I love the hand-touched, history quality of these pieces and remnants.

Another textile technique that is found in the indigo world is shibori, a tie-dye technique where cotton or silk is expertly and finely wrapped with thread then dipped into indigo vats (several times, depending on the desired colour density). You tend to discover this on narrower fabric but it can come in long lengths, especially in cottons.

I was able to visit famous indigo dyer Aizen Kobo in Kyoto and spent an afternoon drinking tea, learning about his craft and having access to his amazing sample books and library.

A small corner becomes a cosy place to
lie around and read, or just dream. To
serve as a backdrop, I painted a dado
about two metres high, bordered with
paper cutouts of red flowers I bought
in Kyoto. It reminds me of the Japanese
inn where we slept on futons, listening
to the river, ate fiddlehead fern and
bathed in natural hot springs.

3

Went through the busiest
intersection in the world.
Lots of umbrellas.
There is even an umbrella
lock-up station.

Everything in Japan has a
place to go and something
to go in: envelopes, boxes,
containers, cloth, chests,
drawers, all size bags.

Dr Seuss trees sit outside
wooden houses with dragon
scale roof tiles.

Spiderwebs covered in morning
mountain dew build on trees
hanging over the river.

WHAT BAMBOO CAN MAKE

SCAFFOLDING
TEA WHISKS
LADLES & SPOONS
MATTING
SCREENS
KITCHEN CEILING
FLOORING
PIPE COVERING
TRAYS
LANTERNS
KITES
BLINDS
TEAPOT HANDLES
TAPS
FOOD
BAGS
BENCHES
BRIDGES
SHOES & SANDALS
UTENSILS
GARDEN TOOLS

Japanese firemen wear heavy
quilt and woven indigo-dyed
jackets and helmet hats. The
reason for this (as the indigo
guy demonstrated) is that
indigo does not burn;
I try it on a white plate and
light a small remnant.

Get thoroughly distracted
by long street of brightly
coloured streamers, floating
decorations. Both sides of
street heavily decorated. So
festive but got super lost.

Gardens planted so
deliberately seasonally

NORTH BY NORTH WEST

COLOUR PALETTE

Bring the colours of your adventures alive: the inky depths of indigo dyes, patched boro & intricate shibori in your range of blues, the neutrals of rice paper & bamboo. The rich reds that stand out in Japanese temples, fire buckets and ceremonies. It creates a classic palette.

[LEFT]
I thought these lights were Chinese, having admired them many times at the store Shanghai Tang. However, after witnessing them at the theatrical dawn fire ceremony in Mount Koya, I decided to include them. Considering the influences of Chinese Buddhism in Japan during the seventh century, it's no wonder they appear in both countries. I love the use of old everyday kimono fabric used for the shade and the glowing ambient lighting it gives off. Layer your patterns with gingham, bamboo blinds, screenprinted coffee sacks and blue screenprinted wallpaper.

I painted this table Pirate Black to give it a strong silhouette.

[THIS PAGE]
Throughout Japan you see copper rainchains that look like flowers and act as downpipes. I have used mine as decoration waiting for the day I have the copper guttering to match. In Japan, they speak of balance in the placement and presentation of objects. It's a harmony that's not symmetrical or matching but a simple, quiet, considered, understated, less-is-more kind of quality. This is known as wabi-sabi.

Mix up your textures: Use leather for flooring and a wooden circle with embossed painted numbers as a tray or tabletop. A perfectly faded flat cushion serves a utilitarian purpose; woven water reed slippers don't need to be worn, but just happen to look the part.

The traditional wooden houses of Kyoto have flooring of tatami mats and low floor-friendly furniture. I have used a layer of raw leather topped with a length of boro to create flooring. Hang your pendant lights low and make sure you have lots of comfy cushions at hand.

This is for eating, conversing, playing games and all your other pastimes.

Your travel inspirations can be incorporated into your interior as quiet moments rather than grand gestures. Here, japonica is applied ikebana-style under a glass dome as a table decoration, providing an intimate memory on a small scale.

Chinoiserie chairs, solid wood table and the back of a seven-fold paper screen provide a backdrop that reminds me of the incredible painted scenes on sliding doors in the temples of Mt. Koya.

[BELOW]
The quietness of a teapot, reminiscent of the elements of a traditional tea ceremony.

41

(ABOVE)
A bundle of hand-dyed thread bought at Aizen Kobo, the
indigo dyer's shop in Kyoto. They are fantastic just
to have, or to use as color references for developing
a palette for your interiors.

(LEFT)
The Japanese use low seating arrangements and shoji
sliding paper screen doors, clever devices to change
the function of their spaces, from sleeping to working
to socializing.

A bamboo table and cushions, all lightweight for easy
moving, sit on a split bamboo mat. A low-hung paper
lantern gives a beautiful soft glow.

[LEFT]
I was inspired from my visit to the amazing Naoshima art island. Consider furniture placement and be aware of its form as well as its function. The ceramic stool, hand-painted photo wallpaper and sculptural base of the table act as art pieces as well as functional pieces.

Even if you cannot have the internal gardens of a classic Japanese house, place a great shaped plant to bring in the green and all its serenity.

[THIS PAGE]
A tonal collection of ephemera picked up in Japan, a lovely reminder of my travels: poetry cards, calling cards and a random 4. I can add and rearrange as I discover more pieces.

Your eyes tell me everything I need to know.

Don't speak. Just let me look at you.

Japanese boro literally means rags and often comes in small pieces, patched and many times mended. Gather as many remnants as you like (I have many!!) and layer them over a lounge to create an overall larger patchwork feel. I love the utilitarian quality of boro as it offers a kaleidoscope of indigo dyes in all its lifetimes.

[THIS PAGE]
When I travel, I look for kitchen
and hardware supply stores. Here, I
added to an ever-growing utensil rack
Japanese hazard tape, wire baskets
and kitchen brushes. Don't hide your
handmade, crafted finds away in the
cupboard — show them off.

It's not about theming your interiors
from one trip, but adding your finds
to your existing collections: a
blue and white Japanese bowl found
at the Tokyo flea market sits with
an Iranian mousetrap my dad gave me,
flashcards from Sandwich, Illinois,
a kingfisher from the south coast of
New South Wales and a past invitation
from a fantastic party.

[RIGHT]
I painted the riser of my stairs
in Cherry Nose red, added a tongue
and groove dado and finished off the
layering with ship rope banister.
This is my interpretation of the
bamboo and knot fencing I had seen in
the temple gardens of Kyoto.

[THIS PAGE]
Old cloth-covered Japanese calligraphy
books make for an interesting texture. Use
them stacked up or open under a glass dome.

[RIGHT]
The Japanese are organized and tidy,
having a place for everything. Don't
feel you need to buy a staired chest — I
recycled balsawood boxes tipped on their
sides and secured (by sheer gravity or
Liquid Nails, if you must). They once
housed old scrolls, paper lanterns, and
ceramics.

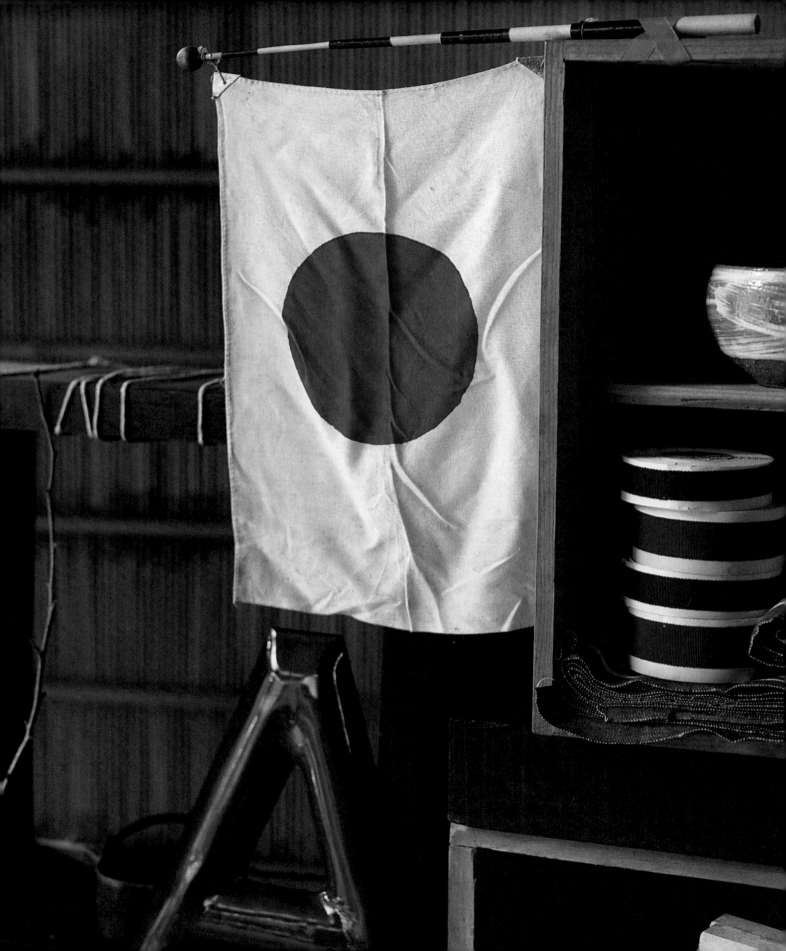

[LEFT]
A miniature fabric Japanese flag is just
taped onto the box, softening up its lines.

[THIS PAGE]
An old sea-crusted sign I spotted as I was
electric-biking around the art island, Naoshima.

Different shaped and sized boxes to hold and
display all your lovely things. This creates
a beautiful, useful display case and can be
casually attached together using small nails
or even hot glue.

The colours of Japan can be the sole
inspiration for your interior.
My favourite Vivienne Westwood
wallpaper panel functions as a
bedhead and sets the tone for a
mix and match of woodblock quilts,
screenprinted and embroidered
pillows. The zen of a Japanese garden
or tea ceremony can be re-created.

55

If you have the luxury of an outdoor shower (but it can be just as easily done inside), pull some things from inside out. Things like this freestanding vintage shaving mirror, a wire soap dish housing Japanese brushes, and a bamboo ladle for scooping water. Heavenly. Create intimacy or texture by leaning up a shoji paper screen door, which doesn't even need to be attached. Neutral tones of the handmade soap and wide-weave cloth make you dream of natural hot sprin in the mountains of Japan.

ITALY 2

ITINERARY

Travelling companion:
my Dad

NAPLES
SALERNO
RAVELLO
POSITANO
SORRENTO

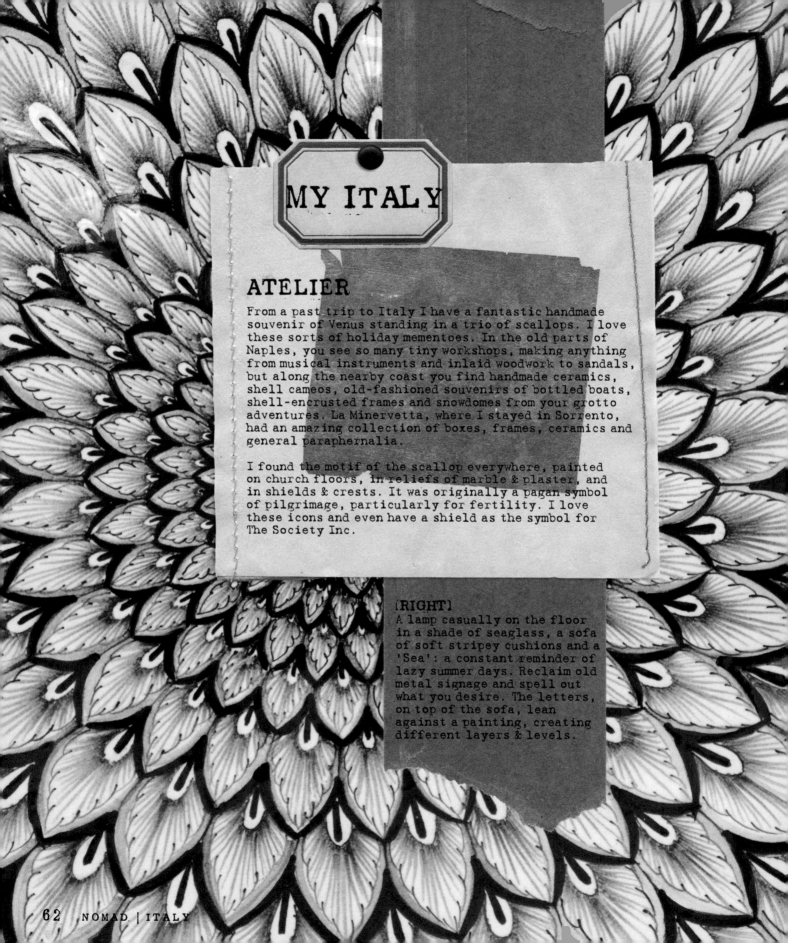

MY ITALY

ATELIER

From a past trip to Italy I have a fantastic handmade
souvenir of Venus standing in a trio of scallops. I love
these sorts of holiday mementoes. In the old parts of
Naples, you see so many tiny workshops, making anything
from musical instruments and inlaid woodwork to sandals,
but along the nearby coast you find handmade ceramics,
shell cameos, old-fashioned souvenirs of bottled boats,
shell-encrusted frames and snowdomes from your grotto
adventures. La Minervetta, where I stayed in Sorrento,
had an amazing collection of boxes, frames, ceramics and
general paraphernalia.

I found the motif of the scallop everywhere, painted
on church floors, in reliefs of marble & plaster, and
in shields & crests. It was originally a pagan symbol
of pilgrimage, particularly for fertility. I love
these icons and even have a shield as the symbol for
The Society Inc.

[RIGHT]
A lamp casually on the floor
in a shade of seaglass, a sofa
of soft stripey cushions and a
'Sea': a constant reminder of
lazy summer days. Reclaim old
metal signage and spell out
what you desire. The letters,
on top of the sofa, lean
against a painting, creating
different layers & levels.

[THIS PAGE]
I painted the edges of books with chalkboard paint, and wrote the titles on the spine with chalk.

[RIGHT]
Put similar materials together — a metal postcard holder sits with a metal mesh lampshade. It's a place for cards, postcards, invites and other ephemera collected on your travels. I cannot help but pick up coasters, wrapping, matchbooks, napkins, maps etc as mementoes.

ULYSSES & THE SIRENS

I have a constant fascination with all things to do with the sea (especially myths). There's a group of three very small rocky islands off the shores of Positano where resided, as legend has it, three sirens whose song lured seamen to an untimely death. Ulysses was keen to hear their song, so had his crew fill their ears with beeswax while they tied him to the ship's mast in such a way that he couldn't free himself. This way, he survived the sirens' song.

65

ZOOLOGY MUSEUM
AND CARAVAGGIO

On a trip to Florence, I came across a huge
Caravaggio exhibition and fell for his story, and
beautiful still lifes of fruit and vegetables. I'd
heard there was a hidden Caravaggio in a church in
Naples, which was part of the reason I wanted to
go there. Due to a poor map, though, I didn't find
it. However, after much up-and-down stairs through
the University of Naples Federico II, I found the
purpose-built zoology museum, almost as good as my
favourite one in Paris. Sometimes, not finding what
you're looking for when you're travelling means you
stumble on something better. Keep an open mind.

Years ago I picked up a fold-out double concertina
book *The Theater of Nature or Curiosity Filled
the Cabinet* by one of my favourite artists, Mark
Dion. It contains line drawings of famous cabinet
of curiosity collections both past and present,
including the famous 17th Century Imperato Museum.
Even though the Museo Zoologico is not quite it, the
skeletons, eggs, shells, nests, stuffed birds and
animals collected in the 1800s are impressive.

My family has a running joke about my luggage being heavy and full of stones. But truly, it is full of stones. This trip was no different — even though I do try to edit it. There's nothing I like more than beachcombing, looking for the perfect pebble, which is grey and egg shaped. I keep my stones on the stairway, in the bottom of the bathtub, in the garden, on the fence, everywhere. I remember where I picked up each one of them.

ROAD TRIP WITH MY DAD

I wanted to do this Amalfi Coast road trip with my Dad, Peter. I believe he was perhaps Italian in a past life, and not just for his sweater, oh-so-casually tossed over his shoulders. He took to the Naples morning peak hour traffic and the hair-raising coastal road with style, expertise and a sense of humour (I had very tense shoulders!)

I love travelling & hanging out with my Dad — he's really funny and enjoys the finer things of life, so this coast was perfect for him and his linen loafers.

[THIS PAGE]
Cotton chenille bedspreads with tassel fringing edge make me think of beach houses and summer holidays. I'm not sure ours, in the Seventies, were as pretty as this one, but my memory often edits out the unattractive things

[RIGHT]
Villa Rufolo in Ravello revealed this arched way, full of dancing light & white on whites that changed colour with the day.

I'd heard of L'Albergo del Purgatorio in Naples, an uber-cool place where, to stay, you have to join to become a friend of Robert Kaplan. He leaves the keys, and the one rule is you have to leave a book or notebook on departure.

You can look into so many
people's lives through the
street eye-height windows.
Soap maker, woodworking
shops, instrument makers
tambourines, weird grotto
things, religious icons,
taxidermy, booksellers.

Modern art litters the walls
and is scattered throughout. -
a mix of new, IKEA and falling
apart furniture.

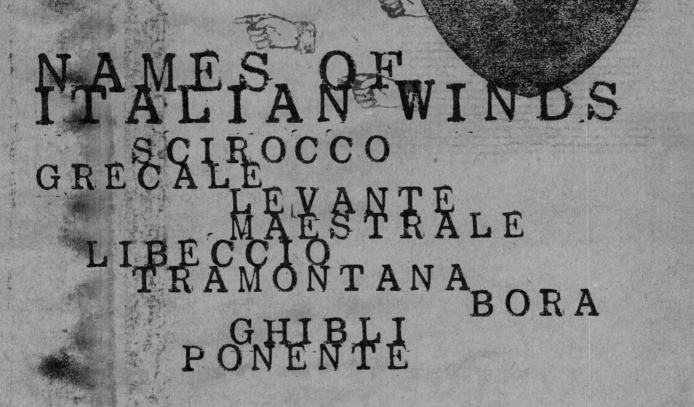

NAMES OF
ITALIAN WINDS
SCIROCCO
GRECALE
LEVANTE
MAESTRALE
LIBECCIO
TRAMONTANA
BORA
GHIBLI
PONENTE

The appearance and placement
of shrines in all sorts of
nooks and crannies, everyday
shrines - an image, a bit
of a saint and a few plastic
flowers.

Mountains fall into the sea.

The consideration of the
vista. The glimpse of a
garden, cloister, view
through a window. What
happens at the end of a room.

TALES OF A SEA GYPSY

☞ COLOUR PALETTE

I am enchanted with all things sea: mermaids & mermen, underwater worlds & treasures, myths & legends, serpents & seafaring spirits. The romance & shimmering beauty of the Mediterranean on the Amalfi Coast in all its magic depths & moods: moon tides, tempests & starry nights.

[THIS PAGE]
I love the immediacy of tape, all colours, all shapes. Put up an idea in minutes and move it around with ease.

Using thin masking tape, I did a crude fish shape (no, I'm not a born-again Christian) resembling the image on the boat that goes from the main port of Positano to Da Adolfo's in the summer months.

Mix it in with your existing collections. A handy ladder that leads to a mezzanine level can be used for books and some of your souvenirs of sea-tossed stones. A plastic urn is my spin on the cliff-clinging sculptures of Ravello.

[NEXT PAGE]
When I loosely hung some rope with knots and loops over a pole, it instantly took me back to the wooden painted boats that go from Positano to the grottos of Capri or potter around the Mediterranean, visiting the water access only inlets and restaurants.

A great entrance and transitional divider as well as conversation starter for any dinner party.

love
is in
the
air

Not everything has to be presented as is. Embellish your flea market find by stencilling a number, and binding the back in rope, which can be found at hardware stores or at auction. It personalises it, and looks great. This was inspired by the wooden fishing crafts of Positano & Capri, all lined up, full of nets, rope & rolled-up canvas in shades of blue.

[LEFT]
I have collected hand-blown glass forever — nothing matches and they all have their own story of the find. This is the time to mix and match and make it casual: porcelain, paper, glass, old doilies, linen all on a background of a handmade lace cloth (I think it was supposed to be a bedspread).

Remember to follow the Mediterranean tradition of siesta, one that all cultures should adopt.

[THIS PAGE]
Say it with love & say it in lights! This will lighten up any occasion and you can write anything.

Just bundle fairy lights together with string or cable tie then mould into your desired word. It's time-consuming, but worth it. Once you've finished, stick it on the wall with the stickiest sticky tape you can find (but not so sticky that it rips the plaster off).

I saw so many roadside and alcove shrines throughout Naples & the Amalfi Coast, often with blue lights as a crown.

Gather all the things that remind you of your trip, like this mantelpiece I saw at La Minervetta (above). For me it was rope, coral, under-the-sea inspired ceramics & flotsam. A great sideboard or foyer display to be a 3-D diary of your fun holiday adventures.

I bought this beautiful book of handmade Amalfi paper & knotted binding from a shop on Capri. Display your finds just on an open page.

pincushion coral

funsale

skeleton shells

ocean tossed
stones

seahorse

tiger eyes

Capri Oct 2010

Pay attention to the details and use the textures and icons seen on your trip: things like a porcelain pendant light, an old steamship towel, rope trivet as a soap dish. Use heavy, extra long tea-towelling linen as a floor mat.

I have a fascination with mirrors; I had one bespoke made in the shape of a shield, similar to ones seen in Sorrento, then layered it in with my vintage collection.

Wallpaper your bathroom with ropes and give it some art — the number 8 is made out of foam and was very inexpensive.

[THIS PAGE]
This simple wicker pendant
sits low beside the bed. I
personalised the store-bought
shade by spray-painting a stripe
(masking the area first in tape)
in the perfect Amalfi blue, just
like one of the wooden fishing
boats beached at Positano.

[RIGHT]
These fabulous number stencils,
from my shop or a stationery
suppliers, can be used over and
over again for the house number
on your front door (oh, to have a
glossy front door in Tales of a
Sea Gypsy), dining chairs or any
other random thing in need of a
bit of decoration.

[THIS PAGE]
Make it festive, make it a fanfare, like the higgledy piggledy narrow back streets of old Naples.

I made this bunting with recycled cardboard, white rope, paint and some stapling. Who wouldn't smile walking through the door with this hanging overhead?

[RIGHT]
Use old-fashioned doilies, linen placemats or tea towels from your great grandmother to line your shelves, then prop away.

I like to mix up what's on the shelf, and place some travel tokens and objets among my books. I bought the metal heart in Naples, in a very cluttered 'antique' shop.

Highlight your bracketed shelves with an accordion clamp light, which can be moved around the house as you wish.

When it comes to interior lifestyle decisions, there are more ways than ever to find inspiration. People around the world now seek ideas from other places, other cultures and other times. They need a single source of reference, a single look at the way the world likes to live. This is

THE WAY WE LIVE

Great Escapes   Around the World

{FOLLOWING PAGES}
For Christmas or any celebration time,
choose your theme and run with it. I
stumbled across a tiny natural history
museum of just four rooms on the island
of Capri.

My theme is based on one room of the
Ignazio Cerio Capri Centre dedicated
to sea flotsam and jetsam: sea urchins,
sand dollars, giant starfish, angel
wings, scallops, razor clams tied
with string, limpets, sea horses,
cuttlefish, nautilus, lobster
and spanner crabs. Loads of other
crustaceans are all housed in wooden
cases on a white terrazzo-tiled floor.
The museum was perched on top of the
hill with the most magnificent view.

Use an old sail as your tablecloth (I
dyed this blue in the washing machine),
and decorate with shells, feathers &
stones. I write on them in pencil, to
remind me where & when I picked them up.

95

[RIGHT]
Bring back the plate rack in a modern way. Mix
your Amalfi Coast ceramics & souvenirs with
your existing pieces & beachcombing finds.

I have used a tangle of metal vines to remind
me of the amazing indoor creeping monstera at
Le Sirenuse in Positano.

Load a tree branch (this one's
a plane) with glittery anchors,
mercury glass & feathered baubles
– all things I saw on my trip.

I love all things shiny & summery!
Throw an alfresco lunch – so Italian.

99

[THIS PAGE]
Pull the inside out and mix with your
deck furniture. A classic canvas canopied
deckchair mixes perfectly with a bamboo
floor lamp & barcart. Campari & soda
please!!!

The coastal spirit comes to you even
if you live in the city.

A giant clam can be used as a vessel for
washing sand from small sandy feet & hands.

[RIGHT]
I was inspired by my room at La Minervetta
in Sorrento. Add to tongue and groove with
a designer stepladder and driftwood star
(a little bit souvenir in style) casually
placed on the counter to get you into the
holiday spirit.

INDIA

ITINERARY

Travelling companions:
Trip 1 Mitzie & Aaron
Trip 2 Sally Campbell

TRIP 1
DELHI
JAIPUR

TRIP 2
JAIPUR
JODHPUR
THAR DESERT

105

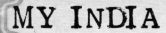

MY INDIA

PILGRIMAGE

My wonderful, beautiful, intelligent mother, Dee, died in 2008 in a desert camp in Rajasthan. This is my own personal pilgrimage to the Thar Desert to the place where her spirit rests and I look forward to celebrating her life.

I carry her longitude & latitude with me for the time when I will have it as a tattoo: N 26°40'35" E 72°19'26"

Manvar desert camp is made up of a scattering of beautiful fabric Raj tents. Set in a semi-circle, the tents each have a verandah sided in bamboo blinds & campaign-style chairs.

The interior is woodblock printed, windows have soft roman blinds, and beds are laden with quilts (and a hot water bottle between the sheets). There's a romantic transparency to it and no hard lines. A place of shadowplay.

My mother was mostly dressed head to toe in some fabulous Brigitte Singh woodblocked outfit, or jodhpurs or an ikat jacket. As I lounge fireside, listening to the desert sounds of a band of local musicians, I think of her and let the beauty & magic of the desert transfix me.

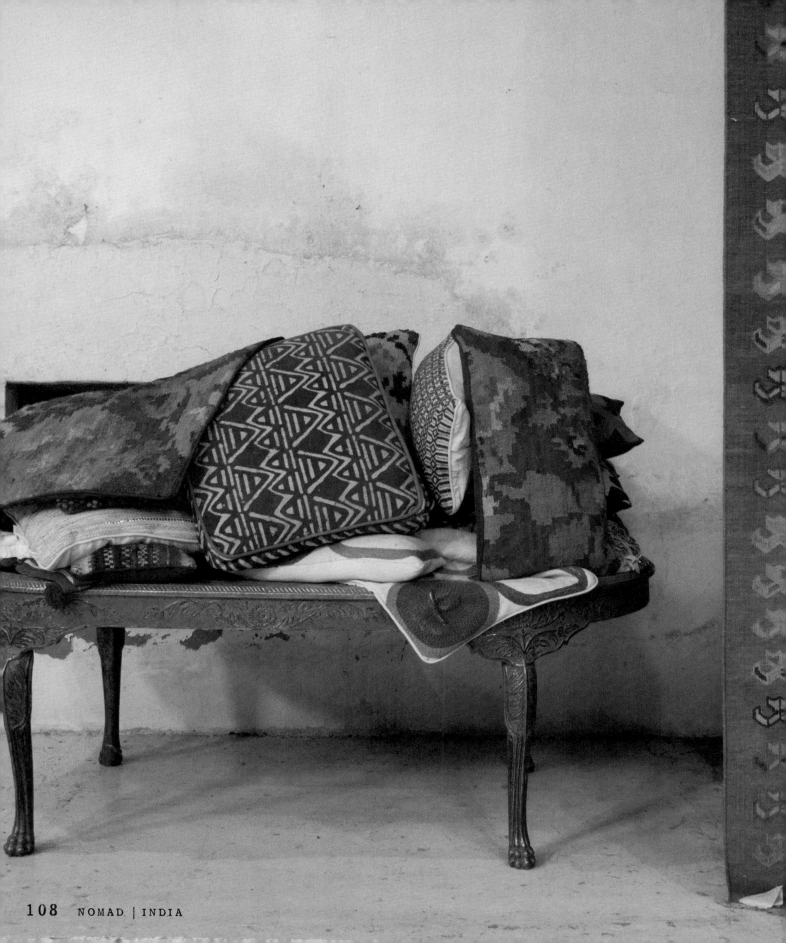

ORIGIN & HISTORY OF TEXTILE NAMES

I have always been interested in the origins of names – visiting the craft museum in Delhi, I came across some extracts from a Levi-Strauss book explaining some Indian ones related to textiles. (Surely jodhpurs stem from Jodhpur!) So many textiles and motifs we use today, like cashmere, paisley, calico and muslin, originated in India, and that was part of the reason I wanted to go there.

Not only are the natural woven textiles so familiar, but so too (even if you don't know all the names) are woodblock prints, beading, metallic threading & weaving, kantha stitching, airiness of khadi, phulkari and aribharat embroidery and so much more. Once you get fascinated & enticed by this, you end up with a large collection of textiles, which I will show you what to do with.

HARDWARE RANGE & TRADES

I work closely with the US store Anthropologie and they asked me to design some decorative hardware pieces for them. As an avid longtime collector of vintage hardware, this was a super exciting project. I met with fabulous craftspeople in Delhi to make this happen. The collection includes many of my fave things – ephemera clips, curious label pulls for your entomological collections, hand-forged nails, rope sconces, wire cage lamps that clamp, all forms of rope drawer pulls, heavy duty wire coathangers, cane-handled scissors and, of course, a canvas & leather toolbag with everything a person needs to style their home.

SALLY CAMPBELL

Every year when I was living in NYC,
I would fly home for a bit of summery
Christmas spirit & family catch-up.
I met Sally Campbell at her bi-annual
textile sale at Shapiro Gallery in
Woollahra on one of my jaunts. We
instantly fell for one another when
I wrapped a tablecloth around myself
and declared it my new scarf! Sally is
fabulous and is usually swathed head
to toe in layers of indigos & reds.
She designs beautiful quilts & cushions
and works directly with natural dyers,
weavers, embroiders & woodblock
printers in Delhi, Calcutta
& Rajasthan.

I jumped at the chance to gallivant &
explore Jaipur with her as my unofficial
guide & companion.

[RIGHT]
Inspired by the endless painted
exterior walls of India and an amazing
cover handmade of remnants, and
casually tossed over a motorcycle in
Samode, patch where you can. I laid
woodblock print samples on the floor
and randomly hung hunting photos, in
mismatched frames, like you see in
Indian hotels & homes.

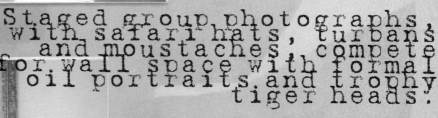

Driving the short distance
to the hotel, I'm already
eagle eyed at the decorated
and painted trucks - shouldn't
all trucks look like this
to brighten up the most
dismal scape.

As we arrived at the factory,
rose petals were rained
down on us and we were
presented with marigold
and chrysanthemum leis.

Staged group photographs,
with safari hats, turbans
and moustaches, compete
for wall space with formal
oil portraits and trophy
tiger heads.

MODES OF
TRANSPORT
ELEPHANT
BUS
STEAM TRAIN
CAMEL (&/OR
CART)
RICKSHAW: AUTO,
CYCLE & HUMAN
IN CALCUTTA
TRACTOR & TRUCKS
HORSE
BICYCLE
HOT AIR BALLOON
1950S AMBASSADOR
WITH CURTAINS
BULLOCKS
DONKEYS
WITH CARTS
VINTAGE CARS

We talked of a wedding last
night. They have people who
carry chandeliers. And white
horse with hot pink painted
hooves.

Coloured paper kites should
be caught in trees more
often.

You notice lots of hidden,
incidental amulets &
talismans above doorways.
The front bumper of cars,
window sills - threaded
with flowers, chillis. I have
seen them with only fresh
things so far.

115

OBJET
TROUVE

COLOUR PALETTE

The dusty, faded colours of India: old paper posters peeling off & covered by new ones, the optimistic paintwork, all faded & chipped, lining streets & shops. Trucks cheerfully decorated with peacocks & swans. Much loved textiles, patched & reworked, dyed turbans of Rajasthan camel drivers, villages freshly painted in celebration of a local wedding.

117

The braid & ribbon store: bedazzled, jewelled sequinned, metallic, typical Indian braids for saris. Lace, cotton & silk, jute rickrack and fringe galore, tassels, beaded ribbon, stripes, gathered, tucked and pinned, leather plaited, crocheted buttons.

TOCCA

BE SAFE • CLOSE COVER BEFORE STRIKING

www.tocca.com

High Class Ribbon
Pon 4298
Nil
N° 3
MADE IN FRANCE

THE
MAGNOLIA
HAIR NET

MADE OF REAL
INDIAN HAIR

INVISIBLE
AND SANITARY

IS
GUARANTEED
IF ANY IMPERFECTIONS ARE FOUND BEFORE
WEARING, RETURN WITH THIS ENVELOPE TO
US AND YOU WILL RECEIVE A NEW NET
The Emporium
DOWN STAIRS STORE
DOUBLE MESH

Strung flowers appear throughout
India, not just for weddings &
celebrations, but for a simple
welcoming & decoration. Apply this
to your own interior and hang from
doorknobs & keys. I used brightly
coloured dahlias.

Soften up wooden & metal furniture
with cashmere throws & cushions.

I love to put framed works outside
even if they have to be brought in
at the end of the day.

(ABOVE)
Get inspiration from a tented
camp or India's many forts.
Set the scene with some draping
& pinning of fabrics, and pile
the bed high with quilts,
fabric & cushions.

(LEFT)
Nothing sets the mood like
candlelight & flowers, scented
or not. Use floor-standing
candlesticks for a more
extravagant effect.

123

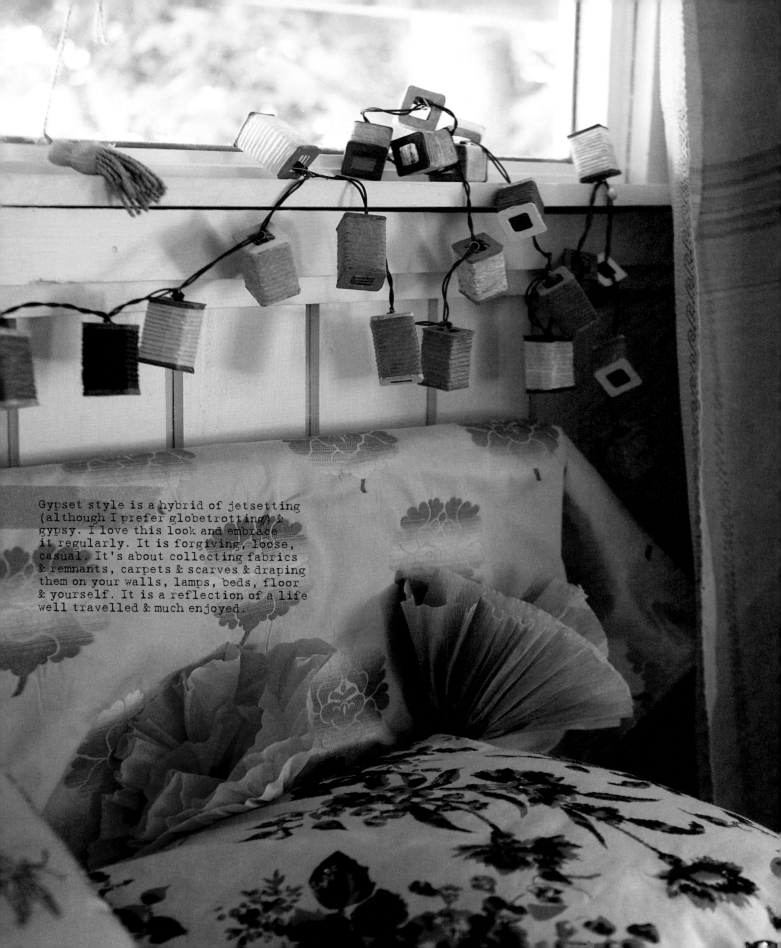

Gypset style is a hybrid of jetsetting (although I prefer globetrotting) & gypsy. I love this look and embrace it regularly. It is forgiving, loose, casual. It's about collecting fabrics & remnants, carpets & scarves & draping them on your walls, lamps, beds, floor & yourself. It is a reflection of a life well travelled & much enjoyed.

(LEFT)
Make it soft, and I mean everything.
Don't be concerned about colours &
patterns, here everything goes. Make
your own fort and display remnants &
quilts picked up on your travels.

(THIS PAGE)
The wonderful roadside houses &
shops make for a very colourful
streetscape. Use the painted finish
patterns; paint a 'panelled' dado or
a stencilled tree of life.

[ABOVE]
Bamboo stick blinds, not too different from the blinds you see everywhere in India, don't only have to cover windows but can soften any unsightly wall or fence.

[LEFT]
Throughout India you see leftovers from the British Empire. I love the mix of both countries – pull in an old fan, add a carved marble elephant and lounge around for the afternoon.

[RIGHT]
Sometimes your purchases can be
bigger than pocket size. If you
really fall in love with India, don't
be scared to ship home doors, columns
& anything else. Purpose build your
interior around them and add your
travel inspiration & purchases.
Create intimate spaces by hanging
sari fabric to create 'soft walls'.

[BELOW]
Mix the simple with the special.
The silver metal chair with plain
white upholstery sits in front of
a peacock & flower motif. If you
need to have a quieter moment,
opt for a neutral palette but keep
the embellishment.

[LEFT]
A play on the trophy heads from Colonial India's hunting past. Make your own plaque shapes from cardboard (old grocery boxes will do) and paint, using your palette of colours.

In India I saw chalk and more permanent painted floors everywhere. I drew a design that washes off when desired and a new pattern applied for another occasion.

[THIS PAGE]
In Delhi, outdoor barbers' shops are as simple as a chair, a mirror on a wall and, hey presto, it's a salon. Apply the same treatment to your outdoor shower.

Cut out colourful patterned paper in triangles and attach to branches to replicate the effect of bunting, like I saw at the Jaipur Literature Festival.

Set the scene with a hand-painted
wallpaper mural as your decorative
backdrop. The life of a maharaja!
Pick a bright base like this blue
hide and add mirrored, embroidered &
embellished cushions and while away
the afternoon. This is similar to the
bolstered floor cushion I lay on as
I listened to the magical sounds of
musicians from the Thar Desert.

[RIGHT]
Use a collection of vintage trophies for
flowers, decorate with a rosette wall and feel
like a winner! It was polo season in Jaipur
when I was there – I had to see a game; that's
where the inspiration for this came from.

[THIS PAGE]
At Samode Palace, a beautiful inner courtyard,
leaf lined with a decoration of objets in an
alcove. A sense of discovery & delight.

It's about calling cards in India.
We await the arrival of one for
the members' stand at the polo.

Pick up old silver cutlery from various places & use randomly – no two sets have to be the same. Instead of a tablecloth, run paper with layers of vintage sari trim down the centre of your table.

Weddings are important
business in India and you
often see white horses with
painted hooves, strings
& strands of threaded
flowers, and parades lit
by chandeliers & their
carriers. Use this theory
& just lie a chandelier
down on the floor or table,
and tangle with fairy
lights if you like for that
crumbling and slightly
chaotic look.

Old sari borders with
metallic thread (don't
fret that they are quietly
disintegrating, that's
the appeal) become a very
romantic Raj table runner.

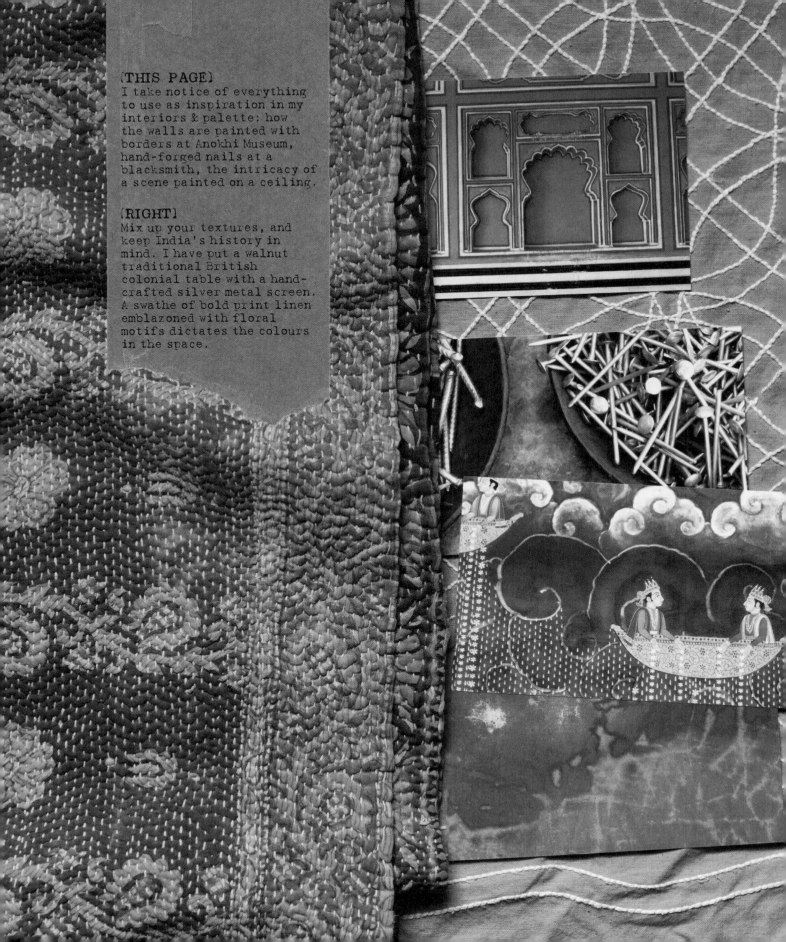

[THIS PAGE]
I take notice of everything
to use as inspiration in my
interiors & palette: how
the walls are painted with
borders at Anokhi Museum,
hand-forged nails at a
blacksmith, the intricacy of
a scene painted on a ceiling.

[RIGHT]
Mix up your textures, and
keep India's history in
mind. I have put a walnut
traditional British
colonial table with a hand-
crafted silver metal screen.
A swathe of bold print linen
emblazoned with floral
motifs dictates the colours
in the space.

[RIGHT]
You can bring everything you admire in India into
your home. The details & patterns that appear in
palaces, on walls & ceilings, and furniture should
not be limited to those things, but continued
through to your tableware. It's nice when it's all a
bit haphazard. I was so surprised when I saw peacocks
running wild and hooting throughout India — even
in the desert. Bring this bird imagery into your
patterns as with this de Gournay wallpaper.

Stencil a lampshade using any paint you have lying
around and with stencils from flea markets.

[THIS PAGE]
Collect lots of sari fabric — cut or use as is for
ends of beds, over windows, as tablecloths, sofa
covers or even as picnic rugs.

145

[ABOVE]
I was ferried out in a rowboat to a small lake palace once used as a post-hunting picnic destination by a maharaja! The hand-carved boat had a horse figurehead.

[RIGHT]
I love this wallpaper with the movement of these horses with wind in their manes. Masks from a party supplier's provide cruelty-free hunting trophies.

SYRIA

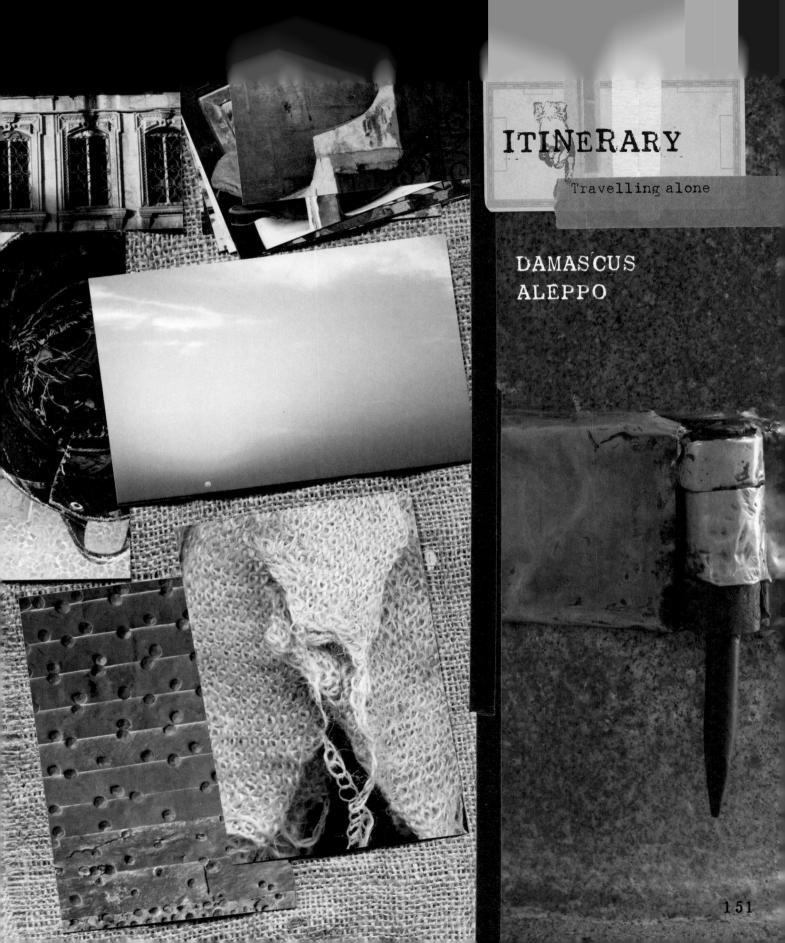

DAMASCUS
ALEPPO

MY SYRIA

THE DAMASCUS ROSE

I first came across Attar of Rose when my
Mum gave me a clear glass vial with corked
top and an old tattered label 'Attar
of Rose'. This had belonged to my great
grandmother and smells so beautifully
of roses I don't believe it has aged a
day! This intoxicating essential oil is
distilled from the fresh petals of Rosa
damascena, or Damask rose, which is said
to have originated in Damascus, Syria.

Since then I have packaged my own
rosewater and cannot stop buying any
perfume or spray that offers this scent.

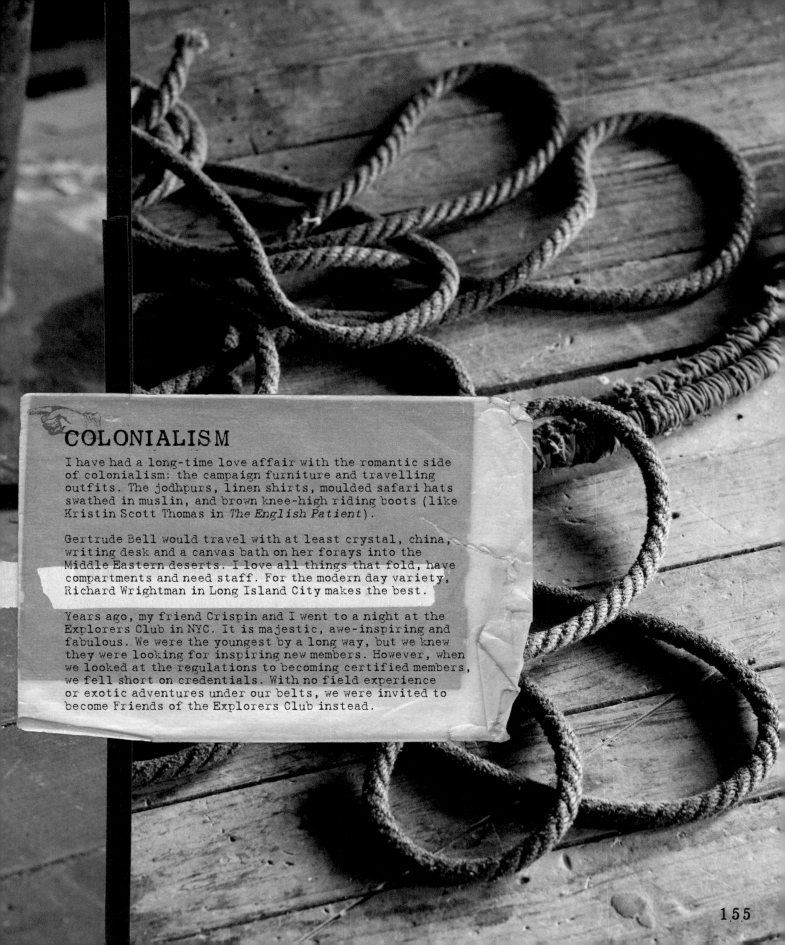

COLONIALISM

I have had a long-time love affair with the romantic side of colonialism: the campaign furniture and travelling outfits. The jodhpurs, linen shirts, moulded safari hats swathed in muslin, and brown knee-high riding boots (like Kristin Scott Thomas in *The English Patient*).

Gertrude Bell would travel with at least crystal, china, writing desk and a canvas bath on her forays into the Middle Eastern deserts. I love all things that fold, have compartments and need staff. For the modern day variety, Richard Wrightman in Long Island City makes the best.

Years ago, my friend Crispin and I went to a night at the Explorers Club in NYC. It is majestic, awe-inspiring and fabulous. We were the youngest by a long way, but we knew they were looking for inspiring new members. However, when we looked at the regulations to becoming certified members, we fell short on credentials. With no field experience or exotic adventures under our belts, we were invited to become Friends of the Explorers Club instead.

AMULETS & TALISMANS

As any good traveller knows, you
need a little extra protection when
embarking on a new adventure. I wear
two amulets, both made from leather,
with various items stitched inside
them to keep me out of harm's way.

In the Seed Souq of Damascus, many
stores are protected with intricate
suspended entanglements of sea
creatures and parts of exotic animals:
pelts of small cats, turtle shells,
small crocs, sharks and puffer fish,
starfish, stuffed birds, antlers
and horns, crabs, porcupine quills,
wolves teeth and other strung pods,
bark and spices.

SILK ROADS OF ARABIA

The Silk Road has always fascinated me. The idea
of continuous travel over thousands of miles for
trade; of people always on the road, only seeing
their families every few years; of the exchange,
over very long distances and thousands of years,
of goods, ideas, knowledge and religion. Romans,
Greeks, Christians, Jews, Armenians and Arabs,
among many others, visited Damascus and Aleppo,
and left permanent reminders of their presence.
There's romance in there, but there's also the
relentlessness of the never-ending journey.

A caravanserai or khan was an inn that offered
weary travellers, pilgrims, merchants and
traders from the ancient trade routes a place to
rest on their very long journeys, feed and water
the animals, purchase new supplies, trade, and
pick up some gossip.

Its layout consisted of a central courtyard with
an entrance generous enough to allow camels and
wares through, with surrounding vaulted 'stalls'
for housing, and occasionally a bathhouse. Many
of these survive today across the Middle East and
other posts of the ancient trade routes and are
often incorporated as market places.

The sound of dice on a wooden
backgammon set makes me want
to while away the hot hours
of the day & drink mint tea.

I'm pleased I bought that old
atlas in Italy - the borders
of the Middle East, I'm sure
have changed, but cities have
not moved.

Starfish, shells, pelts
tortoiseshell, crocs etc
hang above the spice and nuts
stall: talismans and amulets
for sale.

HONEST
MATERIALS

WOOD
LEATHER
SLATE
IRON
STEEL
ROPE
DIRT
PAPER
STONE
CEMENT
HAND BLOWN
GLASS
MUD BRICKS
HAYSTACKS
FELT
CANVAS &
BURLAP

Woodworkers making sieves,
citrus squeezers, spoons,
chairs, chopping boards.

Yesterday I saw the fibres
used to 'knit' the loofah
in the hammam. The freeform
loofah sits with an olive
oil soap in a copper or hand-
beaten bowl. I think I should
buy them all!

Like France and Morocco the
lovely use of the internal
courtyard, sitting and
relaxing in these spaces with
different seating - low and
high, with fountains setting
the background noise.

The famous caravanserai, Khan As'ad
Pasha, in the Damascus souq has the most
magnificent grey & white alternating
courses of basalt and limestone.
Paint your own and casually line up
oversized stencils on the floor against
the wall.

I had the string bag made for me
from heavyweight jute. It's a great
accessory for the daily jaunt around
the souq or to the local grocer's.

Chalk a go-anywhere rug on the floor; it
washes off and can be any size you like!
Find the design in a book or magazine,
and just copy it.

MERCHANTS & TRADERS

COLOUR PALETTE

The colours of the desert are reflected in these oasis towns, all muted neutrals; beaten metal vessels, basalt striped walls of the caravanserai; canvas stretched over roads the width of carts; shiny strong coffee beans & the soft silvery green of olive leaves & pistachios.

[LEFT]
Coffee wafts through the souqs of Damascus
as does cardamom. A recycled coffee sack
from Toby's Estate with all its original
stencilling is personalised by a spray-
painted stencil ampersand. Simply fold
over cushions you already have.

[ABOVE]
The perfume shops of the Spice Souq were
a constant pull for me. I bought amber,
rose and jasmine, among others. House your
spices, bathroom oils and creams, or your
tinctures, in these old-fashioned brown
apothecary bottles.

I labelled them with brown paper, which I
stamped myself.

An exposed bracketed shelf of rough-cut
timber sets the souq-like scene.

[RIGHT]
Have a stack of fabric at hand. I've
gathered mine from around the globe.
Layer them, use them over the back of a
sofa, end of a bed or on the floor: here,
different textures are found in hide,
blanket wool, mohair, mudcloth
and cashmere.

Embrace the romance of Gertrude Bell and imagine how she would have travelled through the desert in the early 1900s (or just watch *The English Patient*). Add a cut of thick industrial felt flooring to cosy you up.

Create a viewing vista that you can look at while you lie down, and create a headboard from a floating bookcase to house your necessities.

torment

I like to display my books,
especially when they have
just arrived in the mail.
This artist, Mark Dion,
inspires me no end and was a
big reason for my travelling
in Italy. A paper whipbird by
my friend Anna-Wili Highfield
adds to the stack.

Shake it up, remember it's not
about theming or being strict
— I can think about Italy and
Syria at the same time.

[FOLLOWING PAGE]
If you don't have built-
ins, a collection of useful,
beautiful baskets do the
trick. Have them on display
for your sheets, towels,
laundry and the like.

Oversized luggage tags made
out of old cardboard and
chalked with their contents
work a charm.

171

[THIS PAGE]
Although the time of
steamships and porters has
gone, the beauty of a linen-
lined trunk with a drawer and
hanging space for a decent
amount of things has not.

Use this well-loved &
globetrotting trunk in your
dressing room or guest bedroom
— a great option for the
necessities, or frivolities
(like a diamond tiara or
feather boa).

[ABOVE]
Use pegboard and make art out of your
collection of beautifully hand-
crafted tools (I have found mine from
many a port, nook and cranny) and
other gadgets, such as a fly swat made
from braided leather and horsehair.
This reminds me of the hardware
and woodworking stores on Straight
Street, or A Street Called Straight,
in Damascus.

[LEFT]
Just because a set of drawers comes
with a handle doesn't mean you have
to stick with it.

A simple knotted piece of old rope
fixed with wire becomes a much better
option with an explorer make-do feel.

[LEFT]
A majestic torn paper and stitched owl isn't quite the falconry of the Syrian desert, but is a hunter nonetheless.

Sculptures come in all shapes and sizes — you often just need to look at something in a different way. A street sweeper's brush topped with a bleached camel bone becomes an artwork in its own right.

(RIGHT)

Ageing paper is the theme, with furniture patterns used on the floor, flashcards as art and a scrunchy blueprint that's not blue. Art doesn't have to be expensive — I used old flashcards and photographs, and either tacked them to the wall, propped them against it or laid them flat to create an installation.

Layers and layers of honest materials: linen, wood, brick.

(THIS PAGE)

The luxury and romance of a suspended potbelly stove. Bring a bit of Syria in with an old oversized coal bucket, hand riveted with a whittled wooden handle, for your kindling and firewood.

I layered a split bamboo mat with knotted wool fabric and a weathered, mended bowl.

I love these textures, they remind me of the mud streets and studded wooden doors of the walled city of Damascus.

in a corner

There
was a
little girl,
Who had a
little curl,
Right in
the middle
of her forehead.
When she
was good,
She was very,
very good,
But when
she was bad,
she was horrid.

wall
w

men
ĕ

I mixed a printed out classic nursery rhyme with flashcards, papier mache initialed "eggs," old photographs (don't you love a mustached man!), a wooden sword, and charts. Not everything has to be attached to the walls; I love things just lying down.

ĭt
ĭ

and
and

floor

bell

can
Can

plum
pl

to

waved

keep

a

tell

then

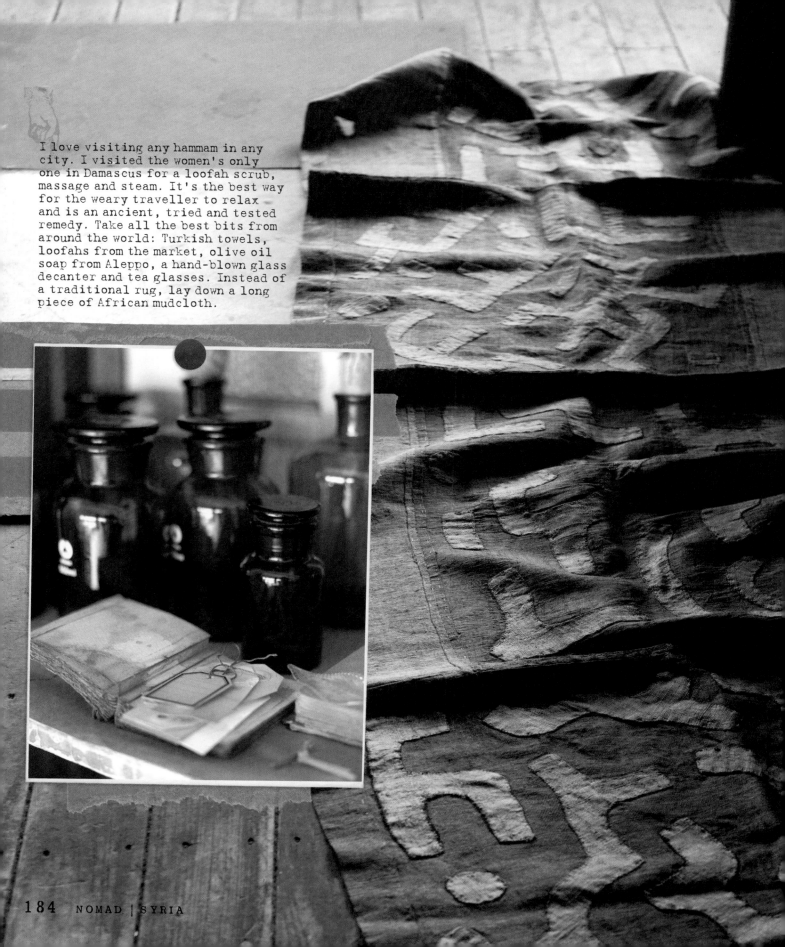

I love visiting any hammam in any city. I visited the women's only one in Damascus for a loofah scrub, massage and steam. It's the best way for the weary traveller to relax and is an ancient, tried and tested remedy. Take all the best bits from around the world: Turkish towels, loofahs from the market, olive oil soap from Aleppo, a hand-blown glass decanter and tea glasses. Instead of a traditional rug, lay down a long piece of African mudcloth.

There's no reason for anything to be ugly.
Consider every aspect of your life, even
down to your cleaning products and how
they're contained. They're so much better-
looking in an old tin bucket and leather tool
bag. Add some handmade scrubbing brushes and
brown-bottled, organic cleaning products,
and cleaning won't seem as much of a chore.

[THIS PAGE]
On the streets of Syria, advertising and signage
is often spray painted & stencilled. This is a
modern take, really embracing some street art.
Keep it mono, keep it lyrical & it looks very much
like wallpaper.

[RIGHT]
Don't try to hide your beautiful bicycle, but
pair it with a leather moulded scooter helmet
(in Japan I saw a girl on a scooter with a velvet
riding hat!)

As I caught the train through the Syrian Desert I saw a scattering of Bedouin tents; this is my version.

A loose linen side-paneled tent has casually knotted leather straps to hold it up. Not only does this look beautiful and romantic, but it is a great way to create intimacy in a loft space. I made mine out of metal poles roped together — it wasn't difficult to do, but if you're not up for it, call in your friendly handyman.

A folding bed fits into the campaign/nomadic lifestyle of camel caravans! Over-scale your light to play on the idea of a traveling gas lantern.

An oversized image I love is printed on
paper at the local office supply shop
for a few dollars and pinned to the wall.
Look for images in antique shops and
markets while you're away and play with
them when you get back. No need to wait
for framing.

Pair with a low-slung leather woven
chair, in which you can sit and read your
Middle Eastern adventure stories.

The teahouses of Damascus are a place to people watch
as well as drink coffee. They're often crowded, so have
a table that folds down.

I stencilled these collapsible chairs and hung them on
the wall with a vintage hook – a great storage solution.

An oversized chequerboard was painted on the floor,
inspired by the great stone courtyards of the mosques.
Google for instructions on how to measure up the floor.

What's not to love about
Glamorous Camping!

Bring some safari style folding
chairs, a metal table and leather
roll-out backgammon set.

Set yourself up with a bucket on a
pulley; fill it with ice and your
favourite wine. Use a small hide
on the ground to glam up any dirt
floor & add a sense of adventure.

Note to self: this can be done at
home, you do not have to be out in
the elements.

MEXICO

ITINERARY

Travelling Companion:
the lovely Katie Dineen

MEXICO CITY

HIP & HAPPENING

While styling in NYC, I stumbled across a company called
DF Casa (DF stands for Distrito Federal and is the local
reference to Mexico City) and was surprised by all the cool
designs I found there. DF Casa represents designers from all
over Mexico who are a real inspiration – my favourite piece
was a white porcelain tree trunk.

I had been reading of the emergence of a young and energetic
art community and wanted to see where the famous Acapulco
chair originated. I wasn't disappointed.

[RIGHT]
Plastic mats which look like rugs (hunt them out at interiors
shops), folding chairs and some flowing stripey fabric sets
the tone with colours and finishes found while bicycling
around the df.

SOMBRERO

DAY OF THE DEAD

I have wanted to experience this for a very long time and the fact that I was going to miss it by five days was devastating. But to know I will witness all the crafts associated with it is exciting. On the Day of the Dead, November 2, the souls of loved ones who have died return to their friends and family, and is therefore a joyous occasion, and not a time for tears. Paper is the medium of choice: Gangly papier mache string-connected skeletons in all sizes, hand-painted and glittered, and brightly painted skulls aplenty, even in candy and chocolate. The word for skull in Spanish is calavera, or calaverita.

FRIDA KAHLO & DIEGO RIVERA

Their lives were so fascinating & fiery, who cannot be intrigued? To maintain their artistic differences both in scale and content, they even had separate living quarters in the house they built in 1931 – so modern both in thought and architecture. Frida cross-dressed & kissed lots of girls.

I'm on the Frida side of the fence when it comes to art, with her constant personal references and intricate symbols.

[RIGHT]
A cool collection of old school maps becomes wallpaper. Hang them randomly as you acquire them.

An old cane daybed gets some new life with a slick of white paint and colourful throws. Use it inside or out.

FOOD.

If only we could get great Mexican food in Australia! I crave bite-size soft tacos with shrimp and guacamole, which I first tasted in NYC, at one of my favourite restaurants, Barrio Chino, on the Lower East Side. I got addicted to those tacos, and the food at Barrio Chino was one of the reasons I wanted to go to Mexico City in the first place.

Even the colour palette of Mexican food is fantastic: limes, chilis, coriander, melon, papaya, cabbage, corn and lemons.

Mexico City is lined with street vendors squeezed into brightly coloured shacks selling fruit juice, mole and tacos, tortillas, guacamole & fajitas. I love the style and immediacy of the street fair, even the wrapping used. The chilis grown in Mexico do not exist in many other places — there is such a distinct flavour and fire.

COCKTELES
LICUADOS
AGUAS

While sitting in the library
at Condesa df, at the Cherner
table with matching chairs,
I found a book of old Mexican
trades: Los Mexicanos pintados
por si mismos.

Frida and Diego's house has
yellow floors, white walls and
green gloss door architraves
with matt green detail above
the door. In Frida's, bottles
of sequins, volumes of Diego's
works and boxed curios.

Votive offerings to cure a
broken heart or a broken leg,
pinned or tied to a shrine.
They're called milagros,
Spanish for miracle.

NAMES OF FLOWERS AND PLANTS

NASTURTIUM
GERANIUM
MARIGOLDS
POINSETTIA
HIBISCUS
BOUGAINVILLEA
SUNFLOWER
BLACK EYED SUSAN
YUCCA
ZINNIA
SALVIA
FUCHSIA
SENECIO
IPOMOEA
DAHLIA
AGAVE
CREEPERS &
CLIMBERS

Went to a market in a cobbled
square in San Angel, still
setting up but bought paper
peonies, some flags, some
skeletons for Day of the Dead.
Amazing paper, a handmade
length with knots.

Everything feels very open
and sunny and spilling onto
the street, and inviting
you in.

All different age groups
drinking coffee, beer,
sangria, playing pool,
and dominoes.

FAVOR DE COLOCAR
LOS PAPELES DENTRO
DEL BOTE DE BASURA
" GRACIAS "

TENDER IS THE NIGHT

COLOUR PALETTE

Mexico DF's people & their lives spill onto the sunny streets: pots of geraniums & marigolds, street stands selling fresh watermelon, tacos & guacamole, grilled corn & salsa verde. Brightly coloured walls & signwriting even the VW & Fifties cars are reds & greens & oranges.

[RIGHT]
Forget faux bois for a moment and
go for a real hand-tooled willow
chair. A super-cool version of twig
furniture in a modern shape. Don't
think of things as forever permanent.
Just-for-the-day impact is fun and
installation-esque.

This looks like a great decorative
background for photo opportunities
at your party — just supply some
props like hats and silly sunglasses
and line up the photogenic subjects.

[BELOW]
Mix it up, make it loud: use an enamel
underplate, organdie napkin and
other crazy stuff just for the fun
of it. Not everything has to make
sense, and each setting can have
its own personality.

Create a classic still life
for your centrepiece; it's
about abundance from your
garden or farmers' market.
Use fragrant nasturtium,
lemons (more than you could
possibly need), lots of
different varieties of toma
and crack open a watermelon.
Don't limit your table to
just the essentials — add
books, and props like an
old artist's palette that
functions as a cutting board

I have rolls of vintage wallpaper,
which I use in all sorts of ways. Line
the inside of a cupboard with something
colourful to create a decorative
background. Create a shelf liner (mine
is out of waxed baking paper), a rather
naive reminder of the paper cut-outs of
the Day of the Dead. Stack with all your
favourite finds — leave the cupboard
door open or even take off the doors.

If you're not ready to wallpaper or paint a wall (or aren't allowed to because you rent), try another tactic. Giant playing cards, available from party suppliers and stuck up with tape, act both as art and wallpaper; mix with patterns, such as caning or palm fronds, reminiscent of the textures seen on your travels.

On your travels, if you stumble across some second-hand bookshops, buy some books. They may not be in a language you understand but stick their pages on the wall at home as a reminder of your discoveries.

Plate 2
MONARCH BUTTERFLY
(*Danaus plexippus*) Female
above Underside
left
Right hindwing Male
upperside,
showing androconia (A)

Plate 3
LESSER WANDERER
(*Danaus chrysippus petilia*)

221

Bring your artwork outside, just for the day. Simply stick it down with masking tape; it brightens up any wall or day.

Lay down some chequerboard vinyl, which you can pick up at a hardware store, to give the space an internal courtyard feel.

[THIS PAGE]
A hanging cane chair reminds
me of sipping cocktails at
sunset on the roof terrace of
Hotel Condesa df.

[RIGHT]
Hang plants in pots on the
wall and watch them grow — to
make a feature, it's best to
stick to one species, repeated
as many times as you can. A
sculptural living wall makes
a great backdrop for an urban
garden or verandah wall.

Mexico is all about indoor/outdoor spaces: plastic
tablecloths, mirrors, frames, potted plants, and
all sorts of homely bits & pieces flow between the
divide as if it didn't exist.

Be green and grow your own kitchen garden. I used
terracotta pots mixed with recycled tomato and
olive oil tins.

Very functional and easy to wipe down, Mexican
oilcloth can be used as a tablecloth, embracing
the vibrancy and colours of the street gardens that
exist throughout Mexico DF.

The DF is a maze of large leafy parks and boulevards
and many of the old houses have window boxes.

[LEFT]
There's no reason mirrors
should only be in bathrooms.
Use them anywhere you like,
even outside, and make a feature
of them, make them large.

A credenza makes this indoor/
outdoor space another room, to
be used all year round.

[ABOVE]
I can't get enough of paper
birds. Here I added one to an
outdoor wall-potted geranium,
super cool. It's all about
accessible outdoor art.

Nº 2

[THIS PAGE]
Simple felt squares in bright colours
are a welcome sight for the eyes — and
gentle on the feet. A direct reference
to my Mexican colour palette.

[RIGHT]
Art comes in all shapes & forms. A
Seventies embroidered picture brings
back the gardens of Mexico City, with
pieces tacked up casually, to be added
to or subtracted from at a whim. Your
bedhead can be art as well.

(LEFT)
made frames out of
cardboard and painted them
with house paint — I use
whatever kind of paint is
close by. Photocopy fave
illustrations or
photos — these are of
bowerbirds and their
nests. Make a collection
and mix up the colours.
Consider your vista; I
love that this screen is
slightly see-through.

(THIS PAGE)
There are so many gardens
in the DF. A bamboo cloche
that would normally
protect seedlings can be
wired up, with the help of
an electrician, to become
a light.

Although the purpose of
this 'flower' pot is to
hold flowers, I love it as
a sculptural objet.

A past assistant made this fantastic mural years ago for a window display in the Flatiron Building. You can do one on paper, but I love that this is on reusable plastic, and has travelled from NYC to Australia. The colours are perfect for Mexico and give this terrace house a cool studio feel.

Don't worry about not having a carpet or rug large enough, add as you go and line them up.

Shrines are hiding in many a nook and
cranny in Mexico, in homes and stores.
I made my own with my trip in mind:
kitsch plastic flowers, a monarch
butterfly made of feathers, cane-
covered candles and other bits, pieces
& memorabilia.

Put it anywhere you like — up high on
a bracketed shelf, on a ledge or in a
quiet corner.

[LEFT]
Inspired by a young artistic community,
where, on every block it seems, an old
mansion has been converted into an art
space (and taking liberty from Rolf
Sachs), I splattered my own furniture
in my paint colours. Furniture you may
find in a studio (I call it 'atelier')
now takes on a more permanent feel.

[RIGHT]
Very Alice in Wonderland, make it fun.
Simply tack oilcloth, with a thin layer
of waterproof foam underneath, to the
top of tree stumps, which you'll have
sourced from a friendly farmer. You'll
find the foam at hardware stores.
Encircle with upholstery tacks, it
doesn't matter if it's a little organic.

Make it festive by simply
tacking up Day of the Dead
paper flags; use a giant yard
game as sculpture (or to use)
and pull your lime green
cowhide outside.

[ABQVE]
Paper cut-outs bought
during the Day of the Dead
celebrations in Mexico City
can be pinned up later, at
home. Flat & easy to pack,
unlike some of my finds.

If you are constantly attracted to the same colours, or just recently inspired by a trip, colour code your accessories. Group cookbooks in similar hues with co-ordinating bits & bobs. Display your super cool kitchen & serving ware on your counter top proudly!

241

MY REFERENCE LIBRARY

I travel with books & other references of relevance (or sometimes of no relevance at all) to wherever I'm visiting. My research & interests expand across books, magazines, music & movies, so as random as it may seem, there is method to the madness in this list.

JAPAN

Old Kyoto: a Guide to Traditional Shops, Restaurants and Inns by Diane Durston
I have had this book for over 15 years in anticipation of visiting Kyoto. A wealth of detailed information on my favourite subjects, trades, among many other things. A must-have.

Lost Japan by Alex Kerr
I was given this by Bodhi, our American guide in Japan (he took us to Mt Koya) who had translated it. A great read on politics, and social & cultural history of Japan.

Food and Travels: Asia by Alastair Hendy
Alastair is a stylist, photographer & writer. This book sings to me, it inspires me to cook. I love that it includes the location & origin of the food — to combine stories & travel adventures with recipes & food pictures is just so appealing.

Katachi: Classic Japanese Design by Takeji Iwamiya & Kazuya Takaoka
I have referenced this heavy book for many, many years. It covers all things Japanese in paper, wood, bamboo, fibre, clay, metal & stone.

POST FOSSIL: excavating 21st century creation, directed by Li Edelkoort
Fab exhibition I went to in Tokyo showcasing modern designs/furniture/home made from wood, leather, canvas, glass, wood & other humble honest materials I love.

Superfuture travelguide
Buy, download, print & make it into your own book with designated folds, cuts & taping.
An up-to-date ubercool travel guide with shops, festivals, what's on, what's hot! www.supercool.com

Lost in Translation directed by Sofia Coppola
I stayed at the Park Hyatt Tokyo just because of this movie and had a private moment at the bar, listening to a saxophonist & looking at night-time Tokyo from a great height. Fab!

ITALY

World of Interiors, April 2009,
Vol 29, no. 4. 'Original Species'
by Jessica Hayns
When I saw this story in my all-time
favourite interior magazine, my
interest in Naples grew even more. I
often travel to a city for a particular
sight, building, shop, exhibition,
restaurant. Nothing like a small
project or pilgrimage.

*The Marvelous Museum: Orphans,
Curiosities & Treasures*: a Mark
Dion Project from Oakland Museum
of California
I adore all this guy's projects (and
his partner, J. Morgan Puett's) and
have seen many in many countries. His
installations & art projects cover
urban archeology, entomologists'
sheds, books, etc

*The Theater of Nature or Curiosity
Filled The Cabinet* by Mark Dion
I bought this small accordion book of
line drawings from Printed Matter, Inc.
in NYC many moons ago. I refer to it
often and it satisfies many a cabinet
of curiosity question.

Ulysses by James Joyce
I have many old copies of this book,
and often think of the adventurer
resisting the lure of the sirens.
However, although it has travelled
distances with this companion, I am
yet to read it! I get swamped & stuck
& put it down.

Images of Distances by Franco Sersale
I bought this at Le Sirenuse in
Positano. The hotel is family owned,
and run by Antonio. This is his
father's book of photography, printed
on beautiful matt art paper. His
photographs are of faces & places in
remote, magical & beautiful ports
around the globe. I feel like ripping
them all out and pasting them on
the wall.

*La Natura Morta Italiana: From
Caravaggio to the 18th Century*,
catalogue from an exhibition at the
Palazzo Strozzi, Florence, 2003
I lugged this massive book home after
being so inspired when I stumbled upon
the exhibition in Italy. I even named a
paint colour Natura Morta which means
still life in Italian.

The Antique & Flea Markets of Italy
by Marina Seveso
I have used this throughout Italy for
fab, hard-to-find markets. A little
hard to navigate if you are not familiar
with the geography of Italy, but worth
the effort.

INDIA

Love Jaipur, Rajasthan by Fiona Caulfield
Not only does this book, with the most beautiful fabric printed cover, come in a fabric bag, but the handmade paper it is printed on is heavenly. The content & points of interest are fantastic. Open it at any page and off you go on a new adventure. I have bought many of these books as gifts.

The Romance of the Cashmere Shawl by Monique Levi-Strauss
Discovered while visiting the Craft Museum in Delhi. A great word & picture reference on the history of textiles (and great for French museum collection information).

British Campaign Furniture: Elegance Under Canvas by Nicholas A. Brawer
One of my favourite types of furniture. Things that fold, are made of canvas, wood & leather, with swathes of netting, and needing trunks & steamships to transport to exotic locations, with staff to construct. You just sit with a G & T. What's not to love!

The Darjeeling Limited, directed by Wes Anderson
As well as just being so funny & crazy, this film has a fantastic colour palette. The fabulousness of the train interior, the brothers' room, the girls' outfits & make-up, the purpose-made orange luggage. It's all great!

The Calico Museum of Textiles, Gujarat, India
I haven't been here yet, but it is so at the top of the list. If you have a love of textiles, this is the place to go.

Indian Summer: A Secret History of the End of an Empire, by Alex von Tunzelmann
I heard Alex (a girl) speak at the Jaipur Literature Festival and was super impressed. She has delved into a controversial subject, from both the Indian & English points of view, with gusto, intelligence & plenty of research. Although it was sold out (congratulations) at the pop-up bookstore, it has been ordered & is waiting to be read.

Thar: The Great Indian Desert
Authentic music of woodwind, string & percussion instruments
To transport me to the nights brazier-side, listening to the desert musicians with their magical guttural sounds in a very, very special place.

SYRIA

Desert Queen: The Extraordinary Life of Gertrude Bell, Adventurer, Advisor to Kings, Ally of Lawrence of Arabia by Janet Wallach
While I was struggling with *Ulysses*, my dad (not a great reader) had bought this book. It could not have been more serendipitous – I was off to Syria, alone. This is jam-packed with history facts, info about the foreign occupation of the Middle East, and the fearlessness & intelligence of an eccentric.

Gulliver's Travels by Jonathan Swift
I bought this in the classic Penguin orange cover edition. It sat beside *Ulysses*.

Mapping the Silk Road and Beyond: 2,000 Years of Exploring the East by Kenneth Nebenzahl
My mum was fascinated by the Silk Road and travelled extensively throughout the countries it traversed. I bought her this book and never thought I would have the adventures she had. How wrong I was!

The Orientalist by Tom Reiss
My mum had started to travel through Azerbaijan & the Caucasus. There is a famous book called *Ali and Nino*. Reiss focuses on this book and looks into the mysterious author behind it, and why this much loved book has had such an influence. I am curious to travel to this part of the world, so my research begins with this.

The Bazaar: Markets and Merchants of the Islamic World by Walter Weiss and Kurt-Michael Westermann
A great reference for what things are made by who & where.

MEXICO

Casa no name by Deborah Turbeville
My Anthropologie friends stayed at
the author/photographer's house in
Mexico. Their pictures were amazing and
inspired me to buy her book. I loved
her collections, colour use, & display
of things.

Volver directed by Pedro Almodovar
I have seen this movie many times. Other
than it being particularly funny and
Penelope Cruz being fab, the interiors
of the houses are really interesting
esp. when Penelope visits her old
village to attend a funeral. The floors
of this place are amazing!

*I will never forget you...Frida Kahlo
and Nickolas Muray* by Salomon Grimberg
I love pics of artists in their studios;
this is no exception and I have coveted
one of these photographs forever.

Frida: A Biography of Frida Kahlo
by Hayden Herrera
Not the greatest book ever written, I
don't think, but covers her fantastic
& fascinating life.

Colour: Travels through the Paintbox
by Victoria Finlay
This is a constant reference in my
library. Great dose of colour history
& origins. It's written in story style,
which holds my interest.

*Infinitas Gracias: Contemporary
Mexican Votive Painting* by Alfredo
Vilchis Roque
Great naive style paintings & images.

Juchitan de las Mujeres by Graciela
Iturbide & Elena Poniatowska
Lent to me by Sally Campbell. Amazing
black & white portrait photography,
of women wearing iguana hats &
traditional costumes.

SHOPS & THINGS I LOVE

MCM HOUSE
20 McLachlan Ave
Rushcutters Bay NSW Australia
2011
Ph 612.9332.2721
Fax 612.9332.2721
sales@mcmhouse.com
www.chuckandbob.com
An edgy mix of vintage French
furniture with cool new wood &
upholstered pieces. Led by the
uncle & nephew team of Charlie
& Rob.

ARMADILLO & CO
www.armadillo-co.com
Perfect flooring for all
lifestyles: woven seagrass
& sisal rugs in neutral,
stripes etc.

EDO ARTS
321 Mona Vale Rd
Terrey Hills NSW Australia 2084
Ph 612.9986.1300
paul@edoarts.com.au
www.edoarts.com.au
Best selection of Japanese fancy
& peasant textiles, many by-
the-yard with backdrop of kimono
chests, porcelain, stone shrines
and other oddities.

**SALLY CAMPBELL
TEXTILES**
Randwick NSW Australia 2031
by appointment only
Mob 0415 403 760
www.sallycampbell.com.au
One of my favourite people
making beautiful things. Sally
works with natural dyers, wood
blockers & weavers in India
to create beautiful quilts,
cushions, tablecloths, curtains
etc. She complements her new
ranges with vintage textile
finds in original form and
reworked.

MARIMEKKO
www.marimekko.com
Classic graphic bold fabrics
& accessories.

GREAT DANE
613 Elizabeth St
Strawberry Hills NSW Australia
2012
Ph 612.9699.7677
www.greatdanefurniture.com.au
Fab new & vintage Danish
furniture & accessories. Have
showrooms in Melbourne and
Brisbane as well.

MY ISLAND HOME
5 Transvaal Ave
Double Bay NSW Australia 2028
Ph 612.9362.8760
www.myislandhome.com.au
Everything you need for a seaside
jaunt & hideaway.

IZZI & POPO
258 Ferrars St
South Melbourne VIC
Australia 3205
Ph 613.9696.1771
www.izziandpopo.com.au
All things Belgian & French,
from shoe racks, porcelain sinks,
huge shop fittings & counters
to small necessary kitchenware.

OUTLIVING
info@outliving.com.au
www.outliving.com.au
Wholesaler of things.

THE JUNK COMPANY
583 Elizabeth St
Melbourne VIC Australia 3000
Ph 613.9328.8121
www.thejunkcompany.com.au
Fab furniture & vintage shop
for drawer pulls, lighting,
industrial furniture &
glassware. Call them & tell
them what you're looking for.
Very reasonable.

JR/SIT
Ph 612.9310.7155
www.jamesrichardson.com.au for
other stockists
Commercial furniture I use for
bars & restaurants. Great range
& quality.

MARK TUCKEY
303 Barrenjoey Rd
Newport Beach NSW Australia 2106
Ph 612.9997.4222
Fax 612.9979.6333
www.marktuckey.com.au for
other stores
Solid wood furniture in great
shapes as well as complementary
modern furniture & accessories.

LE FORGE
59 Denison St
Camperdown NSW Australia 2050
Ph 612.9516.3888
Fax 612.9516.3566
info@leforge.com.au
www.leforge.com.au
Vintage metal, garden, fancy
salvage, wrought iron & French as
well as new ranges of upholstered
& wood furniture & accessories.

MAO & MORE
267-271 Cleveland St
Surry Hills NSW Australia 2010
Ph 612.9699.2700
Mob 0438 226 151
john@maoandmore.com
www.maoandmore.com
All things Asian & cool (as well
as other curiosities of stuffed
animals & paraphernalia). Think
Mao propaganda enamel & ceramic,
fabric lanterns, painted
furniture.

ME TOO PLEASE
2-4 Nelson St
Annandale NSW Australia 2038
Ph 612.9519.2398
Mob 0432 923 004
www.metooplease.com.au
Importers of Mexican oilcloth.

YOUR DISPLAY GALLERY
123 Greenwich Rd
Greenwich NSW Australia 2065
Ph 612.9906.7556
Fax 612.9437.9336
info@yourdisplaygallery.com.au
www.yourdisplaygallery.com.au
A gem I discovered when working
at *Vogue* many moons ago. A
great selection of vintage
hardware, haberdashery, frames,
small pieces of furniture,
kitchenware, books etc.

ANTIQUE GENERAL STORE
2 Warraba Rd
(corner Powderworks Rd)
North Narrabeen NSW Australia
2101
Tel: 612.9913.7636
www.antiquegeneralstore.com.au
I have been frequenting this gem
since my teens. My grandparents
(the hoarder side) lived up the
road. Lots of Australian vintage
furniture and bits & bobs.

JAC +JACK
Ph 612.9380.6630
Fax 612.9380.6693
info@jacandjack.com
www.jacandjack.com
Beautiful hammam towels &
cashmere shawls.

SEASONAL CONCEPTS
122 Redfern Street
Redfern NSW Australia 2016
Ph 612 8399 2435
Mob 0430 044 383
www.seasonalconcepts.com.au
Owned by Ken. A magical, mystical
space of giraffes, flowers,
glass marbles — things old,
forgotten, circus & curious.

OZZIE MOZZIE NETS
29 Barrenjoey Rd
Avalon NSW Australia 2107
Ph 612.9918.0414
Fax 612.9973.1701
www.ozziemozzienets.com.au
I've always had one of these
mosquito nets — beautiful &
simple with a bamboo frame &
cotton netting. Make a world
of your own.

BARBED
Braidwood NSW
antoniathrosby@gmail.com
Great sculptural shapes for
garden or anywhere, made from
salvaged farm barbed wire. Andy
Goldsworthy, eat your heart
out!!

SIMPLICITY
25 Violet St
Revesby NSW Australia 2212
Ph 612 9774 5855
Fax 612 9774 3569
info@simp.com.au
www.simp.com.au
Great curtain tiebacks
& trimmings.

IVY & ALL ITS FRIENDS
330 George St
Sydney NSW Australia 2000
Ph 612.9240.3000
www.merivale.com
Coolest restaurants/bars &
hottest function spaces in town
(& the world!) Including lots
I've designed.

GARDEN LIFE
357 Cleveland St
Surry Hills NSW Australia 2016
Ph 612.8399.0666
Fax 612.8399.0655
www.gardenlife.com.au
My friend Richard's uberchic
garden store with cafe. Great
plants & pots, & outdoor stuff.

SPINNEYBECK
Distributor in Australia:
Gabrielle
61.407 900 825
www.spinneybeck.com
Best source of manipulated hides
& leather: think dyed cowhides
in a large selection of colours,
perforated leathers & the like.
Great resource for upholstery
& flooring.

DAY OF THE DEAD
A celebration of loved ones past
November 1 & 2 throughout Mexico.

ANNA-WILI HIGHFIELD
www.annawilihighfield.com
Commission only
Most beautiful paper sculptures
in the world. My owl flies above
my bed.

COLLETTE DINNIGAN
Ph 612.9361.0110
www.collettedinnigan.com.au
Most beautiful dresses ever,
both fancy & not.

TOBY'S ESTATE
www.tobysestate.com.au
for locations
An Australian coffee staple
now taking over Williamsburg
& NYC areas.

DE GOURNAY
de Gournay representative
in Australia
alice@degournay.com.au
www.degournay.com
Spectacular hand-painted
wallpapers & fabrics. My
favourites are the banana leaf,
murals, birds & flowers: perfect
for anything from ballrooms
to bathrooms.

SIMON SZENES
417 Illawarra Rd
Marrickville NSW Australia 2204
Mob 0416 777 084
celebratesimon@gmail.com
Industrial stuff from salvage
to furniture — nothing too small
or too big!

TOKYO BIKE
1 Marys Place
Surry Hills NSW Australia 2010
Ph 612 9357 1223
www.tokyobike.com.au
Seriously uberchic bikes.
You choose your frame and pick
all your accessories.

YARDGAMES
Ph 612 99381713
www.yardgames.com.au
Giant games for outdoors, hours
of entertainment.

HOTELS I STAYED IN

LE SIRENUSE
via Cristoforo Colombo 30
84017 Positano
Italy
Ph 39 089 87 50 66
Fax 39 089 81 17 98
info@sirenuse.it
www.lesirenuse.com
A family hotel full of antiques
& heirlooms. Once the family
holiday house, it oozes style
& elegance.

L'ALBERGO DEL PURGATORIO
Palazzo Marigliano
via San Biagio dei Librai 39
80138 Naples
Italy
Ph 39 081 299 579
nhsp@aol.com
This is a treat. You have to
become a member, and it's worth
the effort. Rambling rooms, you
could have a large party here and
everyone could stay.

LA MINERVETTA MAISON
via Capo 25
80067 Sorrento
Italy
Ph 39 081 877 4455
Fax 39 081 878 4601
info@laminervetta.com
www.laminervetta.com
Red, white & blue, a hillside
over the Mediterranean — what
more could you want. Not only is
the interior spectacular: blue
& white stripe tiles and coastal
ceramics, but the breakfast is
delicious as you contemplate
life on the sunny patio. A very
personal collection of hand-
picked furniture pieces lovingly
restored & souvenirs collected
from around the globe. Very bold
& graphic.

VILLA CIMBRONE
via S. Chiara 26
84010 Ravello
Italy
Ph 39 089 857 459
Fax 39 089 857 777
info@villacimbrone.com
www.villacimbrone.com
I stayed here years ago in a blue
& white tiled room. Spectacular,
established gardens set high
on the hill, looking over the
Amalfi Coast.

CONDESA DF
Av. Veracruz N.102
Col. Condesa 06700
Mexico D.F.
Ph 52 55 5241 2600
Fax 52 55 5241 2640
contact@condesadf.com
www.condesadf.com
Super cool with fab food, set
around a central courtyard.
A turquoise, black & white
interior, do not miss the private
library with a great selection
of books, & the roof terrace for
sunset drinks. Get a room looking
over the tree-lined streets.

OKUNOYU RYOKAN (JAPANESE TRADITIONAL INN)
Kurokawa Onsen
Minami Shokoku-cho
Aso-gun
869-2402 Kumamoto-ken
Japan
Ph 0967 44 0021
Traditional Japanese rooms,
dotted through the maples, with
an energetic river alongside.
A tatami-matted room serves as
your dining room cum sleeping
quarters. We dined on a 36-plate
meal (all tiny beautiful morsels
of everything) then slept in
a row on futons. Plenty of hot
pools to choose from: one in the
room, men's, women's, communal
& private!

BENESSE HOUSE/LONG ROOM

Gotanji, Naoshima, Kagawa
7613110
Japan
Ph 81 (0)87 892 3223
Fax 81 (0)87 892 2259
naoshima@mail.benesse.co.jp
www.benesse-artsite.jp/en
benessehouse
A hotel in a museum, what a
fantasy. Designed by Tadao Ando,
this James Bond-like structure
looks over the Seto Inland Sea.
And my room is beautiful, looking
over the many scattered islands.

SAH AL NAUM

Baghdad St, Ekeibeh
neighbourhood, Amara,
Damascus, Syria
Ph 963 11 231 08840064
info@sahalnaum.com
www.sahalnaum.com
An old merchant's house reworked
as a rambling guest house built
around a courtyard in which to
lounge. Run by the hip Ahmed,
who lives on the property with
his fiancee and can make
anything happen! Amazing
Middle Eastern breakfasts,
and always interesting guests
to converse with.

LOHARU HOUSE

Civil lines, Jaipur
302001 Rajasthan, India
Guest house, with rooms set
around gardens, and run by the
lovely Begum Fauzia Ahmad Khan
and Aimaduddin Ahmad Khan. Dinner
is served at 8.30 – 9pm — the
food makes you view Indian food
differently and, quite frankly,
ruins you for anyone else's.
There is always an interesting
bunch at the table, including
writers, directors, politicians,
high commission staff, designers
etc. Very old salon style.

MANVAR DESERT RESORT & CAMP

Khiyansaria
Jodhpur-Jaisalmer Highway
Distt. Jodhpur, Rajasthan, India
Ph 9129 282 680 11, 268911
Mob 9194 1407 0491
www.manvar.com
It takes an hour and a half to get
from Jodhpur to the camp, and all
the way you're driving through
the most amazing desert. The
tents are luxurious, and there
are camel rides and jeep safaris
to be had, or you can do nothing
more energetic than listen to
music and watch the sunset.
Beautiful.

COOL PLACES

ZOOLOGICAL MUSEUM
Via Mezzocannone, 8
80134 Naples
Italy
Ph 081-2535204; 081-2535212;
www.musei.unina.it
Tens of thousands of insects;
taxidermied specimens hundreds
of years old, a massive whale
skeleton and even some extinct
animals. Lots of mother of
pearl too.

DIEGO RIVERA & FRIDA KAHLO STUDIO MUSEUM
Calle Diego Rivera 2, corner
of Altavista
Delegacion Alvaro Obregon
CP 01060
Mexico
Ph 55 50 15 18
www.estudiodiegorivera.
bellasartes.gob.mx
I'm a huge fan of Frida Kahlo
and her paintings. Nice little
homage to a great & interesting
artist. Not so excited by Diego's
paintings but love that they
lived in separate houses, joined
by a walkway.

NAITO
Sanjo-ohashi
Nishi-zume
Nakagyo-ku
Japan
Ph 075 221 3018
Kyoto shop, run by the same
family for over 100 years, making
and selling traditional wooden
brooms. They are all natural
fibres, and include your regular
square indoor broom, ones for
geisha make-up, paintbrushes,
nailbrushes and all sorts of
shapes to get into unusual
places, nooks & crannies. All so
lovely, it would be rude to hide
them in the shed or cupboard.

AIZEN KOBO
Omiya Nishi-iru
Nakasuji-dori
Kamigyo-ku
Japan
Ph 075 441 0355 (English spoken)
Fax 075 414 0355
www.web.kyoto-inet.or.jp/people
/aizen
Indigo dyer's studio, house &
shop in Kyoto. All three are
lovely if you are lucky enough
to get invited in! Shibori and
indigo dyed fabric by-the-yard,
paper, clothes and thread for
purchase.

TOKYU HANDS
Tokyo
www.tokyu-hands.co.jp/en
for stores.
Everything you need for any
& every craft, and more.

AL JOUBAILI SOAP FACTORY
Sh Bab Qinnesrin, across from
Bimaristan Arghan
Old City Aleppo
Syria
Walk back a few hundred years
into this ancient working olive
oil soap factory. Soap is only
made in the cooler months. If
you're there at any other time
of year, you can pop in for a
tour and buy some to take home.

KHAN AL-NAHASEEN
(Khan of the coppersmiths)
Aleppo
Syria
Only open on Fridays from 1pm,
or maybe Friday morning
– it's confusing.
Or by appointment, make well
in advance through the Belgian
Consulate, 362 2666
I couldn't get access (not even
with bribes) and was bitterly
disappointed. I hope you have
more luck, it sounds fabulous.
Privately owned since the
nineteenth century by the
Poche family, who have vast
collections of antiquities,
photographs, archaeological
finds & mosaics, maintained by
Madam Jenny Poche.

ORIENT HOUSE ANTIQUES
1st floor Saahat al-Hatab
Aleppo New City
Syria
Jam-packed with lots of metal
things. I bought some amazing
door knockers, tin tambourines &
pulls as well as some photographs
of moustached men – all fitted
into a vintage leather satchel.

HAMMAM AMMOONAH
Women only
Baghdad St Behind Al Dahdah-
Bawabet Al Aass
Damascus
Syria
Ph 963 11 23 16 414
I love hammam and try to visit
one whenever I can. I do however
avoid the rather aggressive scrub
they offer.
For me, it's about steaming,
soaking, breathing & relaxing.
Great for tired travelling bones!

EL KHATEEB
In souq al-Bziuriyya (spice
souq)
Damascus-Bzourieh
Syria
Ph 963 2222811
The most beautiful old wooden
shop with apothecary glass-
fronted drawers, lots of glass
stopper bottles of essence.
Take your time choosing your
favourite scents and take home
in small vials.

JODPHUR TAILOR
9, Ksheer Sagar Hotel
Motilal Atal road
Jaipur
India
Ph 98290-56691, 93515-84026
For your handmade bespoke
jodhpurs, breeches & riding
jackets.

ANOKHI CAFÉ
Jaipur
2nd Floor, KK Square
Above Crosswords Bookstore
C-11 Prithviraj Rd, C-Scheme
Jaipur 302005
India
Ph 0141 4007244
If you need some salad and a
non-Indian food break, go here,
it's worth the wait. Definitely
try the cake — it will get you
through the Jaipur traffic!

JAIPUR LITERATURE FESTIVAL
jaipurliteraturefestival.org
I was lucky enough to co-ordinate
my January dates to Jaipur with
this. A very casual low-key vibe,
pop in & out as you please. It
is free and held in the grounds
of the beautiful Diggi Palace
where you can also stay. Small
& intimate with a pop-up Full
Circle store (best bookshop
in India). After a couple of
days you feel free to start up
conversations and introduce
yourself to people who interest
you. This is where I had my
picture taken and put in the
Jaipur newspaper social pages.

JANTAR MANTAR
Jaipur
These giant 3D zodiac charts
& sundials make it seem as if
you're walking in a de Chirico
painting. The architecture,
light & shadows at this
astronomical observatory are
beautiful & mesmerising.

SATAYAM
Laxman Dwara
City Palace
Jaipur
India
Ph 0141 260 1434
This was a last stop in Jaipur
on the way to airport and is a
must. Lightweight towels, khadi
scarves, kerchiefs — superior in
quality, which is reflected in
the price. I left with a lovely
stack of things.

A BIG THANK YOU TO

Brother/photographer extraordinaire Chris, Donna Hay,
Edwina McCann, Reuben Crossman, Leta Keens, Aaron Hoey
& Mitzie Wong, Hannah Brady, Leah Rauch, my Dad, and
the team at Murdoch.

The Tuckeys, Collette Dinnigan, Justin Hemmes,
Michelle Leslie, Adam Zammit, Simon Szenes, Karman &
Paul of Edo Arts, Sally Campbell for lending me their
beautiful spaces to create my interiors!

All the assistants who helped and sweated through
the hot month of January in Sydney.

And all the other globetrotters, shop owners,
chefs & cooks, camel drivers, safari men, train &
ferry captains, lumberjacks & hoteliers, mapmakers,
vendors, surveyors & field journalists who made my trips
so interesting and remarkable.

First published in 2011 by Murdoch Books Pty Limited

Murdoch Books Australia
Pier 8/9
23 Hickson Road
Millers Point NSW 2000
Phone:+61 (0) 2 8220 2000
Fax:+61 (0) 2 8220 2558
www.murdochbooks.com.au

Murdoch Books UK Limited
Erico House, 6th Floor
93-99 Upper Richmond Road
Putney, London SW15 2TG
Phone:+44 (0) 20 8785 5995
Fax:+44 (0) 20 8785 5985
www.murdochbooks.co.uk

Publisher: Diana Hill
Designer: Reuben Crossman
Photographers: Chris Court, Sibella Court
Editor: Leta Keens
Production: Alexandra Gonzalez

Text copyright: Sibella Court 2011
The moral right of the author has been asserted.
Design copyright: Murdoch Books Pty Limited 2011
Photography copyright: Chris Court, Sibella Court
2011

National Library of Australia Cataloguing-in-
Publication entry

Author: Sibella Court

Title: Nomad: Bringing Your Travels Home

ISBN: 978 1 74266 013 4

Subjects: Collectibles in interior decoration.
Travel paraphernalia. Interior decoration.

Dewey Number: 747

A catalogue record for this book is available from
the British Library.

Printed by 1010 Printing International Ltd in
2011. PRINTED IN CHINA. Reprinted in 2011

Colour separation by Splitting Image Colour
Studio, Melbourne, Australia.